Oracle Disk I/O Tuning
Disk IO Performance & Optimization for Oracle Databases

Mike Ault

I would like to dedicate this book to the brave men and women in the United States Armed Services. Having been in the Navy myself I understand their sacrifices during peace, as well as during war time. These men and women give their lives so that our freedoms are protected. I give them my respect and my thanks.

- Mike Ault

Oracle Disk I/O Tuning
Disk IO Performance & Optimization for Oracle Databases

By Mike Ault

Copyright (c) 2004 by Rampant TechPress. All Rights reserved.

Printed in the United States of America.

Published in Kittrell, North Carolina, USA

Oracle In-Focus Series: Book #15

Series Editor: Don Burleson

Production Manager: Linda Webb

Production Editor: Teri Wade

Cover Design: Bryan Hoff

Printing History: June, 2004 for First Edition

ISBN: 0-9745993-4-4

Library of Congress Control Number: 2004101895

Table of Contents

Using the Online Code Depot

Your purchase of this book provides you with complete access to the online code depot.

The scripts in this book are available in zip format and located at the following URL:

www.rampant.cc/io_disk.htm

Throughout the text, scripts in the code depot are named and called-out in a box like this:

⊞   **myscript.sql**

Once you have downloaded the code, you should easily be able to locate and run your scripts. If you need technical assistance in downloading or accessing the scripts, please contact Rampant TechPress at info@rampant.cc.

Get the Advanced Oracle Monitoring and Tuning Script Collection

The complete collection from Mike Ault, the world's best DBA. Packed with 590 ready-to-use Oracle scripts, this is the definitive collection for every Oracle professional DBA.

It would take many years to develop these scripts from scratch, making this download the best value in the Oracle industry.

It's only $39.95 (less than 7 cents per script!)

To buy for immediate download, go to

www.rampant.cc/aultcode.htm

Conventions Used in This Book

It is critical for any technical publication to follow rigorous standards and employ consistent punctuation conventions to make the text easy to read.

However, this is not an easy task. Within Oracle, there are many types of notations that can confuse a reader. Some Oracle utilities such as STATSPACK and TKPROF are always spelled with CAPITAL letters, while Oracle parameters and procedures have varying naming conventions in the Oracle documentation.

It is also important to remember that many Oracle commands are case sensitive, and are always left in their original executable form, and never altered with italics or capitalization.

Hence, all Rampant TechPress books follow these conventions:

Parameters - All Oracle parameters will be *lowercase italics*. Exceptions to this rule are parameter arguments that are commonly capitalized (KEEP pool, TKPROF), these will be left in ALL CAPS.

Variables – All PL/SQL program variables and arguments will also remain in lowercase italics (*dbms_job, dbms_utility*).

Tables & dictionary objects – All data dictionary objects are referenced in lowercase italics (*dba_indexes, v$sql*). This includes all *v$* and *x$* views (*x$kcbcbh, v$parameter*) and dictionary views (*dba_tables, user_indexes*).

SQL – All SQL is formatted for easy use in the code depot, and all SQL is displayed in lowercase. The main SQL terms (select, from, where, group by, order by, having) will always appear on a separate line.

Program names – Programs and code depot script names are always in *lowercase italics*.

Products – All products that are known to the author are capitalized according to the vendor specifications (IBM, DBXray, etc). All names known by Rampant TechPress to be trademark names appear in this text as initial caps. References to UNIX are always made in uppercase.

Acknowledgements

I would like to acknowledge the hard work that the folks at Rampant Tech Press have put into getting this book ready. My thanks go out to Linda, John and all of the other folks who have worked hard to bring this book to light.

Mike Ault

Preface

Since back in the days when the choice was SQLDBA or nothing (version 6), Oracle has come a long way with its database monitoring tools. Server Manager, Enterprise Manager, and the numerous other Oracle-provided monitoring tools make the task of monitoring databases easier.

However, there are still limitations. Many of these tools only monitor the top level of the data dictionary. They can tell the DBA how many users, tables, and indexes are active, but they provide little information about deeper operations, such as user activity or table activity.

Several companies offer excellent monitoring tools: Precise, with its Q and Precise*SQL packages, the Quest product suite, Patrol from BMC, ECO Tools, and the many CA offerings spring to mind. These tools are liberating for some DBAs, but others are crippled by their lack of knowledge about the underlying structures of the data dictionary. Every DBA needs to understand the data dictionary before he or she can manage these complex, feature-laden tools.

Tools are only as effective as the person using them, and a DBA has to be able to dig into the data dictionary to find and correct problems. Some may believe great tools make great works, but try giving the best materials and tools to ineffective or inexperienced workers. The result may be better than with poor materials and tools, but it will probably still be unsatisfactory. As with all things, when using Oracle, knowledge means power - the power to solve problems, or better yet, to prevent them from happening in the first place.

In the past few years, the author has interviewed dozens of candidates for Oracle DBA and developer positions. Some had great resumes, but they were nevertheless uncomfortable under the Oracle hood. Many were clueless about the workings of the data dictionary or the *v$* tables.

The data dictionary tables (usually suffixed with a dollar sign ($)) are owned by the SYS user, and normally should not be accessed, except when the supporting views don't have the required data. Oracle has instead provided *dba_*, *user_*, and *all_* views of these tables. They should be used whenever possible. Oracle has also provided the dynamic performance tables (DPTs), which provide running statistics and internals information. These DPTs all begin with *v$* or, in their pristine form, *v_$*. The DPTs are documented in the Oracle reference manual for your version of Oracle. In RAC environments, if you wish to see all RAC instance data, use the *gv$* views which contain data for all RAC instances for a specific database.

The data dictionary views are created by the *catalog.sql* script, located in the $ORACLE_HOME/rdbms/admin directory. The *catalog.sql* script is a required readme file. The script has numerous remarks and comments that will significantly improve your understanding of the data dictionary views. But be forewarned, the *catalog.sql* script is over 200 pages.

Disk Architecture

Introduction

In many ways, database professionals view disk tuning as not required, not necessary and simply not in their job description, taking whatever is given them from the system administration area and making the best of it.

If we are truly concerned about database performance (overall system performance in general), we, as database professionals, must get more actively involved in disk architecture and tuning efforts. Most tuning efforts in the disk arena are aimed at file serving. By file serving, I mean getting an entire file served to a single user as quickly as possible. Unfortunately, the file serving model is woefully inadequate for database systems. Database systems tend to have many single point reads (random reads) mixed with some large reads (sequential) and in some cases, very large reads (direct reads). This mixed IO profile for databases causes issues if the disk IO subsystem is not properly tuned to handle database needs.

In much of today's modern architectures, there are several layers of abstraction between the database and the physical disks. In fact, it is safe to say the days of individual disks being used to support a production database are, for the most part (except for very small systems), gone. Now, disk subsystems consist of arrays of disks commonly called RAID, which stands for redundant array of inexpensive disks (although some substitute interchangeable for inexpensive). They provide the needed IO bandwidth to help with performance as well as providing redundancy for disk failure mitigation.

The DISK array is usually sliced up by a controller into what are known as LUNs (logical units) and these LUNs are then used to create the logical volumes upon which we place our virtual disks. Usually there is at least one layer of abstraction (disks-LUNS) and at least two (disks-LUNS-logical volumes). These layers of abstraction make pinpointing disk performance issues difficult and may cause masking of symptoms. Sometimes there is a third level of abstraction, RAID, where multiple logical disks are sliced into relatively thin (8k to 1 megabyte) stripes and then combined to form RAID arrays. Figure 1.1 illustrates this, up to the logical disk level.

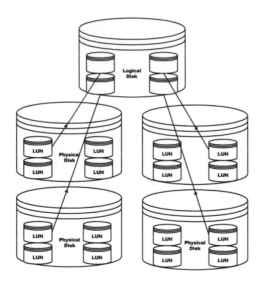

Figure 1.1: *From Disk to LUN to Logical Disk*

To visualize the RAID level on top, picture multiple logical disks sliced into thousands of sub-disks and then recombined into a RAID disk set. Many times, database administrators are asked about their underlying disk arrays, and they profess to have absolutely no knowledge of the disk arrays beyond the mount points and maybe the RAID level (more about RAID levels in later chapters).

As you can see, tracking a disk performance problem from a database file to the underlying RAID volume, to the logical disk, to the LUN and finally to the physical disk level can be daunting. Further complications arise by some automated tuning features of the more advanced arrays where stripes or LUNs may be migrated from "hot" physical disks to cooler ones. Luckily, many RAID manufacturers are now providing graphical interfaces that track IO and other performance metrics down to the physical disk level.

As you can see from the very general discussion above, disk array tuning is not a trivial issue. Hopefully, in the chapters that follow, you will come to understand the issues surrounding disk tuning and you will learn how to optimize your disk array system for your database needs.

General Disk Architecture

In the general sense, disk architecture hasn't changed much in the last seventeen or so years. Disks have gotten smaller and faster, but their general features have not changed that much. Disks are physical entities consisting of some dimensionally stable substrate overlaid (usually aluminum alloys, but now magnesium and even glass or ceramics are being considered) with a thin layer of material that can take and hold a magnetic charge. Optical media uses laser gouged pits to indicate zero or one rather than the presence or lack of magnetic signals; the mechanical technology is essentially the same in either magnetic or optical media. This general magnetic disk structure is shown in Figure 1.2.

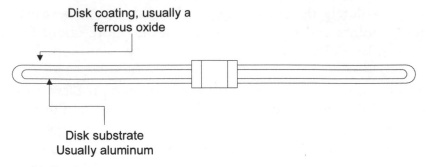

Figure 1.2: *General magnetic disk structure*

For a magnetic disk, an electromagnet is used to place or remove magnetic charges to the magnetically sensitive coating. These magnetic charges are later read by a read head that senses the magnetic charge. Naturally, the closer to the disk that the head flies, the weaker and thus, denser the signals can be.

On an optical disk, the substrate is usually an optically clear plastic with one side coated in a material that is photosensitive to a particular wavelength of light (like that given off by the laser used to encode it). The laser burns small pits in the photosensitive material that corresponds to the digital signal provided to drive the laser. Later, a laser that is non-harmful to the photosensitive material is used to read the pits. Figure 1.3 shows the general structure for optical media.

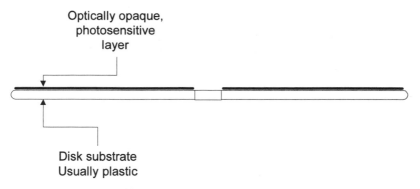

Optically opaque,
photosensitive
layer

Disk substrate
Usually plastic

Figure 1.3: *Optical Media Structure*

In both magnetic and optical technologies, the read-write heads are usually combined into one device, which is mounted on a mechanical assembly that moves the read-write heads back and forth above the media as the media rotates at high speed. In a 10,000 rpm magnetic disk, the disk edge is moving at over 100 mph for a 3 ½ inch drive. On high volume drives there may be several platters that have magnetic media on both sides as well as dual read/write heads. The magnetic material is applied using a vacuum deposition method, allowing for a very thin and uniform layer. The magnetic media is then overlaid with a thin carbon and a lubricating layer.

On a magnetic drive, the read-write head moves on an actuator arm that actually makes an arc as it reads from the inner to outer edge of the disk. On an optical disk, the read-write head moves in a track and moves linearly from the inner to the outer edge. This is demonstrated in Figure 1.4.

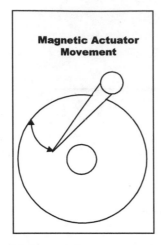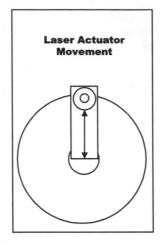

Figure 1.4: *Magnetic verses Optical Head Movement*

Read and write times for magnetic drives are usually an order of magnitude faster than for optical drives. This speed difference indicates that optical drives are good for archival, but not for live data.

Since disks are mechanical devices, they are subject to the laws of physics. The laws of physics determine how fast things can move in relation to each other and also determine how the air flows over and around a rotating object. All of these factors combine to limit the upper speed that a disk can rotate as well as how fast the actuator can move the heads back and forth over the disk surface. The rotational speed and arm or track speed determine the various latencies associated with either a magnetic or an optical disk drive. The rotational latency is related to the speed at which the disk rotates. There is also the positional latency, which is mostly determined by how fast the disk actuator can move. These combined latencies form the basis for the seek times for the drives. Seek times generally determine how fast data can be retrieved from a specific disk.

With a magnetic drive, the read/write head(s) float over the disk surface on the long actuator arm. Sudden physical shocks can cause the actuator arm to flex, causing the read-write heads to momentarily make contact with the disk surface. The effects of the read-write heads coming in contact with the surface of a disk vary from little damage and no loss of data to a severe disk crash with loss of all data unless sophisticated and expensive disk recovery processes are used. There have been instances of disk failures (head crashes) where the magnetic media was gouged off down to the aluminum substrate.

In Optical drives, the distance between the read/write laser and the disk must be held fairly fixed, thus the disk is locked into a drive mechanism and the laser is rigidly mounted in a head that travels by way of a track mechanism. The chances of a head crash in a laser disk system are virtually nil. Obviously, any scratches in the optically clear plastic substrate may result in the data on the photosensitive substrate becoming unreadable. Likewise, any scratches that remove the optical media also result in data loss. As long as the recording media is unharmed, an optical disk can be re-polished to remove surface scratches or blemishes on the optically clear plastic side, there is no way to repair the disk if the photosensitive media side is damaged.

💻 **Code Depot Username = book, Password = disk**

Disk Layout

Disks are laid out using circular tracks to store data. Unlike the grove on a record (there is only one, it is a huge spiral from start to finish), the tracks on a disk are true circles, each independent of the other for the most part. On multi-platter disk drives (multiple platters on the same spindle with multiple arms and headsets), the tracks are grouped into cylinders with the tracks that line up on each of the platters grouped together. The data in each track is further broken down into sectors where each sector contains the same number of bytes. The tracks on a disk get longer as you move out from the center, therefore the number of sectors increases per track. Tracks are grouped into zones where each zone of tracks contains the same number of sectors. This disk layout is shown in Figure 1.5.

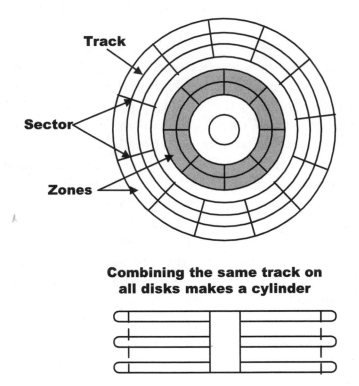

Combining the same track on all disks makes a cylinder

Figure 1.5: *Disk Layout*

Disk Logic Boards

In the beginning, disk logic boards provided the means to position the heads to specific addresses for read and write activity. As the technology matured, logic boards added capabilities, and now the logic boards also optimize reads and writes to minimize the head motions required. The logic boards also monitor head speeds, temperatures and other physical characteristics to better enable the placement of heads as components expand and shrink due to temperature and other ambient conditions.

Cache and Disks

Even with the recent speed improvements in disk technology, the disk drives are still the slowest component (other than tape drives) in the computer system. Let's look at the basic math. A 1-GHz CPU (central processing unit) (slow by today's standards) equates to 1 billion operations per second. At best, memory operates approximately at 20 million-plus memory operations per second. What about the hard disk? Even fast disks have average access times of greater than five milliseconds per unit of information off the disk; that equals a maximum, given the absolutely optimal conditions of 200 operations a second. Usually, you are doing well to get close to 100 operations a second with less being the norm. This means CPUs at 1 billion operations a second, memory at 20 million operations per second, and disks at 200 operations a second. Obviously, the disk can be a severe performance bottleneck in a computer.

Even high-speed server drives have a seek time greater than four milliseconds, which means it can only perform around 250 operations per second under ideal conditions. While this speed is better than what used to be available, it is still too slow when processors are running at over 2 GHz. One way to speed up operations is to store the most recently accessed data in a special memory area known as cache. Most modern drives now come with several megabytes of cache per drive.

Generally speaking, you want data cached as close to the disk drive as possible.

Cache algorithms utilize optimistic read-ahead logic and write logic that optimizes for most general types of computer operations (read into this statement, file serving) however, unless properly set up and tuned cache operations can cause significant issues for databases.

Disk Performance Statistics

When you review disk performance statistics provided by the manufacturer you will get a table that looks something like Figure 1.6.

PHYSICAL SPECIFICATIONS	
Formatted Capacity [1]	250,059 MB
Interface	1.5 Gb/s Interface (Serial ATA 1.0)
Bytes Per Sector (STD)	512
User Sectors Per Drive	488,397,168
Dedicated Landing Zone	Yes
Actuator Latch/Auto Park	Yes

PERFORMANCE SPECIFICATIONS	
Data Transfer Rate	
- Buffer to Host	150 MB/s [2]
- Buffer to Disk	748 Mbits/s max
Average Read Seek	8.9 ms (average)
Track-to-Track Seek [3]	2.0 ms (average)
Full Stroke Read Seek [3]	21 ms (average)
Average Latency	4.2 ms
Rotational Speed	7200 RPM
Read Cache	Adaptive

PERFORMANCE SPECIFICATIONS	
Write Cache	Yes
Buffer	8 MB
Drive Ready Time	9.0 sec (average)
Start/Stop Cycles	50,000 minimum
LBA Support	Yes
Error Rate (non-recoverable)	<1 in 10^{14} bits read

1. Western Digital defines a megabyte (MB) as 1,000,000 bytes, and a gigabyte (GB) as 1,000,000,000 bytes.

2. Effective maximum transfer rate running Serial 1.0.

3. On reads and writes.

4. 20% duty cycle.

5. No non-recoverable errors during operating tests or after non-operating tests.

6. Half sine wave measured in 2 ms duration, measured without isolation.

7. Sound power level.

8. Three-year standard warranty on WD Caviar Special Edition hard drives. This standard warranty may be subject to variations imposed by local law or regulations.

Figure 1.6: *Typical Drive Specifications*

(Provided courtesy of Western Digital Corp. www.westerndigital.com)

So what do these statistics mean? The first section of Figure 1.6 shows the layout for the drive giving formatted capacity, almost (why drive manufacturers insist on not using the standard values for megabytes and gigabytes is a mystery), the interface speed, bytes per sector and number of sectors. This section is fairly self-explanatory. What we are really interested in is the second section of figure 1-5 where they provide actual performance statistics.

In the second section of Figure 1-5, the following statistics are provided:

- Data Transfer Rate(s) - This is broken into two parts, disk buffer to host and disk buffer to disk. Notice how the disk buffer to host is 150 MB/s (megabytes per second) while the buffer to disk is specified as 748 Mbits/s max (megabits per second). If you are using 32 bit bytes (most modern systems are, if not 64 bit), then this means a transfer rate of around 23 Mbytes per second to disk.

- Average Read Seek - Anytime you see seek, think actuator arm movement. This statistic is telling us on the average how long it takes the actuator arm to position itself for a read of a sector.

- Track-to-Track Seek - Again, this deals with actuator arm movement and tells us the average time for movement when the arm is already positioned over a specific track and must move to a different track.

- Full Stroke Read Seek - This tells us how long it will take for a read if the arm is positioned in the absolute worst position when it receives the move command.

- Average Latency - Generally, when you see latency you are speaking of the amount of time it takes for the proper sector to rotate into position under the read/write head once the read/write head is in position. The faster the drive rotates the lower the latency numbers should be.

In general, seek times are controlled by how fast the arm on the actuator can move. This is controlled by the power of the actuator mechanism and the weight of the actuator arm and read/write heads. The more powerful the disk actuator and the stiffer/lighter the actuator arm the lower the seek times.

Latency is controlled by rotational speed of the disk. The higher the disk speed the lower the latency.

Some disk companies also provide expanded statistics, for example Figure 1.7 shows the specifications provided by Seagate for their Cheetah series of drives.

CHEETAH 10K.6 - TECHNICAL SPECIFICATIONS	
DESCRIPTION	
Model Number	ST3146807FC
Model Name	Cheetah 10K.6
Form Factor (width)	3.5-inch
Form Factor (height)	1-inch
PHYSICAL SPECIFICATION	
Height	25.4 mm
Width	101.6 mm
Length	146.05 mm
Weight	0.73 kg
CAPACITY/INTERFACE	
Formatted Capacity	146.8 Gbytes
Interface Type	40-pin SCA
PERFORMANCE	
Internal Transfer Rate (min)	475 Mbits/sec
Internal Transfer Rate (max)	841 Mbits/sec
Formatted Int Transfer Rate (min)	43 Mbytes/sec
Formatted Int Transfer Rate (max)	78 Mbytes/sec
External (I/O) Transfer Rate (max)	200 Mbytes/sec
Avg Formatted Transfer Rate	66 Mbytes/sec
Average Seek Time, Read	4.7 msec typical

CHEETAH 10K.6 - TECHNICAL SPECIFICATIONS	
Average Seek Time, Write	5.3 msec typical
Track-to-Track Seek, Read	0.35 msec typical
Track-to-Track Seek, Write	0.55 msec typical
Average Latency	2.99 msec
Default Buffer (cache) Size	8,000 Kbytes
Spindle Speed	10,000 RPM
Spinup Time	20 sec
Number of Disks (physical)	4
Number of Heads (physical)	8
Total Cylinders	49,855
Bytes Per Sector	512
Areal Density (Mbits/sq in)	36,000 Mbits/square Inch
Track Density (TPI)	64,000 tracks/inch
Recording Density (BPI, max)	570,000 bits/inch

Figure 1.7: *More Detailed Specifications from Seagate*

Seagate has added the average write seek times as well as giving formatted transfer rates. This gives a more complete picture of the disks abilities. Notice that Seagate has also included the number of disks and cylinders as well as the number of heads. The number of heads indicates that the platter is two-sided and both sides are being used for data. The four platters this Seagate drive provide 8 tracks per cylinder (2 on each disk, an upper track and lower track).

However, the biggest factors in single disk performance will be the disk speed and speed of the actuator arm as measured by the average latency (rotational latency) and seek times. More platters in a drive will do little to improve write or read time for database related IO. The number of platters is more related to capacity since the read/write heads are generally not independent but are mounted on a single actuator with multiple, parallel arms. This means that only one disk surface is read from or written to per operation, but multiple operations may take place in a single IO.

This dependence on the rotational speed and actuator arm speed is what limits the IO capability of the drives. Comparisons of multiple drives from the same company shows that while the number of platters/sides used determines the capacity of the drive, the IO rates and seek and latency values remain fairly constant. Figure 1.8 shows this for multiple Seagate drives with the same speed disk but different capacities.

CAPACITY AND INTERFACE				
Formatted Gbytes (512 bytes/sector)	40	80	120	160
Interface	Ultra ATA/100	Ultra ATA/100	Ultra ATA/100	Ultra ATA/100
PERFORMANCE				
Internal Transfer Rate (Mbits/sec)	683	683	683	683
Max. External Transfer Rate (Mbytes/sec)	100	100	100	100
Avg. Sustained Transfer Rate (Mbytes/sec	>58	>58	>58	>58
Average Seek (msec)	8.5	8.5	8.5	8.5
Average Latency (msec)	4.16	4.16	4.16	4.16

Multisegmented Cache	2048	2048	2048	2048
Spindle Speed (RPM)	7200	7200	7200	7200
CONFIGURATION/ORGANIZATION				
Discs/Heads	1/1	1/2	2/3	2/4
Bytes per Sector	512	512	512	512
Logical CHS	16383/ 16/63	16383/ 16/63	16383/ 16/63	16383/ 16/63

Figure 1.8: *Platters Effect on IO, Latency and Seek times*

To get the same effective IO rate per gigabyte of capacity when going from a single-side, single-platter 40 gigabyte drive to a four-side, dual-platter 160 gigabyte drive, you would need four or more of the 160 gigabyte drives (100/40=2.5 MB/sec/GB verses 100/160= 0.625 MG/sec/GB)! This is the little secret that undermines the entire "bigger is better" myth of disk capacity.

Disk Capacity - The Double-Edged Sword

While data transfer rates from disks have grown in direct proportion to disk speed, disk data capacity has been growing exponentially. This results in a double-edged sword that cuts us if we only plan for volume by reducing our IO capacity, or cuts us budget wise if we really plan based on IO needs. What this means is that while the amount of data we can store has been increasing on a per-disk basis, the speed at which we can access that data has decreased. For example, look at Table 1.1.

Max Capacity	Drives/terabyte	Average Access Time (msec)	MB/s/ Drive	Transfer Rate (total)
9 gig	112	9.9	8.5	952
18 gig	56	7.7	14	728
36 gig	28	5.4	23	544
73 gig	14	5.6	33	462
180 gig	6	4.16	58	348

Table 1.1: *Comparison of IO Capacity Verses Drive Size*

To achieve the same IO capacity as we had with our 112-9 gigabyte disks, we would need to buy 2.7 (952/348) times the needed capacity of 180 gigabyte drives even with their superior access times and MB/s transfer rates. The values in Table 1.1 reflect the performance values when that drive capacity was the maximum available. Of course, as we saw in Figure 1.7, if we replace the old 9 gig drives with the new 40 gig (36 gig formatted) drives with the sustained transfer rate of 58 MB/s we get 28*58 or a total transfer rate of 1624 MB/s, which would require 28 of either the new 73 or 180 gig drives in order to match the IO rate from the 28-40 gig drives.

Watch out for the double-edged sword!

Therefore, if we used the new 40 gig drives, we cold expect better IO transfer rates of up to 70 percent based on IO rate, while if we bought the 180 gig drives based on storage capacity alone we would see a decrease in IO capacity of over 270%. This is why IO capacity should be the driving factor in disk drive purchase, not storage volume per disk.

Recent research shows that the more loaded a disk drive is (volume wise) the poorer it performs; generally speaking, you should shoot for only filling drives to at most 50-60 percent of their total capacity.

It all boils down to knowing the expected IO rate from your database and planning the number of disk drives based on the required IO rate, not only on the amount of space required, or you could find yourself volume rich but IO capacity poor. In addition, don't plan to get exactly the volume of disks you need, to get maximum performance, double that number allowing for only a 50-60 percent by volume usage.

Conclusion

Disk technology hasn't really changed in the last 20 years. The basic, platter, motor, actuator and arm and read/write heads are all still there, however, their size has dramatically decreased (there used to be 10 megabyte platters that where 12-14 inches in diameter, they would stack these in "cake boxes" that you could remove from drives, the first Winchester drive required a rack mount and two men to carry it, capacity: 90 megabytes) the speed of the drives has increased and their volume capacity has grown almost exponentially (from 30 or so megabytes for a single-surface, single platter, to 40 gigabytes for a single-surface, single platter drive). However, the disk IO rate has grown fairly linearly rather than exponentially, thus it has not kept up.

This exponential storage volume growth and linear IO rate growth has resulted in less IO capacity for a given volume of drive capacity, and we have to plan for this when we size our drive arrays.

References

www.westerndigital.com

www.seagate.com

Exploring Disk Size and Oracle Disk I/O Performance, Bruce D. Rodgers, *Oracle Internals*, June 2001, Copyright 2001 CRC Press LLC.

Hard Disks and How They Are Organized, Drew Robb, Auerbach Publications, Copyright 2003 CRC Press LLC

Disk Interfaces

Exploring Disk Interfaces

Disk drives by themselves are fairly useless. Even if they are connected to power and are spinning along nicely, they will do little good unless they are attached to your computer system through a disk interface. Disk interfaces are based on standards, which ensure, if a manufacturer follows the interface specification, any computer that supports that interface, or has an interface card that supports the interface, can talk to and control the drive.

"Don't forget the disk interface!"

Essentially, there are three main types of disk interface in use today (I have excluded USB due to speed and capacity restrictions):

ATA - Advanced Technology Attachment, originally known as IDE or Integrated Drive Electronics. The usual ATA bus accepts two drives, a master and a slave. The ATA specification has been expanded to include ATA-2, ATA-3 and SATA (Serial ATA). Serial ATA will only accept one drive but has a smaller cable and higher speed. ATA doesn't support hot swapping of drives and has limited array capabilities.

SCSI - Small Computer System Interface - This is a bus independent standard for system level interfacing between a computer and intelligent devices. The original SCSI has been expanded to include SCSI2 and SCSI3 and can have up to 16 devices per channel (wide) or 32 devices (very wide). SCSI supports hot swapping of drives. SCSI is designed for being used in an array.

IEEE1394 (Firewire) - An interface originally designed for use in the MAC/Apple environment but has gained in popularity in the PC realm as well. Firewire is a high performance serial bus specification. The IEEE1394- Firewire specification has recently been upgraded to significantly improve the Firewire bandwidth (400 Mbit/sec to 1 Gbit /sec), Firewire supports up to 126 devices per channel.

Fibre Channel - usually considered a subset of SCSI, provides for up to a 2-Gigabit/sec data transfer rate and is generally used when communicating to a large disk array with multiple SCSI channels.

Each of these, as indicated, may have multiple implementations with new and improved features. Table 2.1 shows a comparison of the speed of various types of disk interfaces.

INTERFACE	SPEED
Serial	115 kb/s
Parallel(standard)	115 kb/s
Parallel(ECP/EPP)	3.0 Mb/s
SCSI	5-320 Mb/sec

INTERFACE	SPEED
ATA	3.3 - 133Mb/sec
USB1.1	1.5 Mb/s
USB2.x	60 Mb/s
IEEE1394(b)	50-400 Mb/s
Original IDE	3.3-33 Mb/sec
SATA	150 Mb/s
Fibre Channel	2 Gb/sec

Table 2.1 *Comparison of Disk Interface Speeds*

Let's examine the major interface types in more detail.

ATA Interface

ATA is short for Advanced Technology Attachment. ATA is a disk drive interface that integrates the controller on the disk drive itself. There are several versions of ATA, all developed by the Small Form Factor (SFF) Committee:

- ATA: Which is also known also as IDE, supports one or two hard drives per cable, a 16-bit interface and PIO (Parallel IO) modes 0, 1 and 2. ATA is also IDE, which is an abbreviation for either Intelligent Drive Electronics or Integrated Drive Electronics, depending on who you ask. The IDE interface is an interface for mass storage devices, where the controller is integrated into the disk or CD-ROM drive. Although it really refers to a general technology, most people use the term to refer the ATA specification, which uses this technology.

- ATA-2: This ATA mode supports faster PIO modes (3 and 4) and the multiword DMA modes (1 and 2). ATA-2 also supports logical block addressing (LBA) and block transfers. ATA-2 is usually marketed as Fast ATA and

Enhanced IDE (EIDE), which is a newer version of the IDE mass storage device interface standard developed by Western Digital Corporation. ATA-2 will support data transfer rates in a range of 4 and 16.6 MBps, about three to four times faster than the old IDE standard. In addition, it can support mass storage devices with capacities of up to 8.4 gigabytes, whereas the old standard was limited to 528 MB. Due to its lower cost, enhanced EIDE has replaced SCSI in many areas. EIDE is sometimes referred to as Fast ATA or Fast IDE, which is essentially the same standard, developed and promoted by Seagate Technologies. It is also sometimes called ATA-2. There are four EIDE modes defined. The most common is Mode 4, which supports transfer rates of 16.6 MBps. There is also a new mode, called ATA-3 or Ultra ATA, which supports transfer rates of up to 33 MBps.

- ATA-3: Minor revision to ATA-2.

- Ultra-ATA: Also called Ultra-DMA, ATA-33, and DMA-33, ultra-ATA supports multiword DMA mode 3 running at up to 33 MBps.

- ATA/66: A version of ATA proposed by Quantum Corporation, and supported by Intel, that doubles ATA's transfer rates to 66 MBps.

- ATA/100: An updated version of ATA/66 that increases data transfer rates to 100 MBps.

- Serial ATA: Often abbreviated SATA or S-ATA, it is an evolution of the Parallel ATA interface. Serial ATA is a serial link -- a single cable with a minimum of four wires used to create a point-to-point connection between devices. Transfer rates for Serial ATA begin at 150MBps. One of the main design advantages of Serial ATA is that it has thinner serial cables that facilitate more efficient airflow inside a form factor and also allow for smaller chassis designs. In contrast, IDE cables used in parallel ATA systems are bulkier than Serial ATA cables and can only extend to 40cm long, while Serial ATA cables can extend up to one meter.

Serial ATA supports all modern ATA and ATAPI devices (ATAPI is short for AT Attachment Packet Interface, an extension to EIDE (also called ATA-2) that enables the interface to support CD-ROM players and tape drives.) The major limitation to SATA is that it only supports one device per cable. The differences between ATA and SATA are shown in the following diagram. Essentially, ATA allows two devices per ATA connector that are configured in a standard Master-Slave setup, while SATA only allows a single device per connector. ATA allows up to 66 Mbits/sec per connector while SATA allows 150.

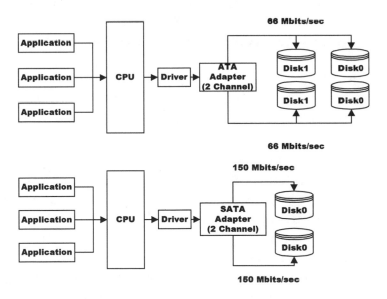

Figure 2.1: *Comparison of ATA and SATA Interfaces*

SCSI Interface

SCSI is an acronym that stands for small computer system interface. Usually it is pronounced "scuzzy." SCSI is a parallel interface standard used by:

- Apple Macintosh computers
- PCs (IBM compatible)
- UNIX systems
- LINUX Systems
- Some Proprietary Systems

The SCSI interface is used to attach peripheral devices to computers. SCSI interfaces provide for faster data transmission rates (up to 320 megabytes per second in SCSI3) than standard serial and parallel ports. In addition, you can attach many devices to a single SCSI port (8 to16), so that SCSI is actually an I/O bus rather than just an interface.

Even though SCSI is an ANSI standard, there are several variations of it, so two SCSI interfaces may be incompatible. For example, SCSI supports several types of connectors.

While SCSI has been the standard interface for some computers, others come with only IDE and IEEE1394 (firewire) or USB, less expensive interfaces, in which the controller may be integrated into the disk or CD-ROM drive. Other interfaces supported by PCs include enhanced IDE (EIDE) and ESDI for mass storage devices, and Centronics for printers (although fewer and fewer systems are providing Centronics interfaces). However, you can attach SCSI devices to a PC by inserting a compliant SCSI board in one of the expansion slots. Many new high-end PCs or Intel based servers come with SCSI built in. However, that the lack of a single, accepted SCSI standard means that some devices may not work with some SCSI boards.

SCSI comes in the following varieties:

- **SCSI-1:** Uses an 8-bit bus, and supports data rates of 4 MBps

- **SCSI-2:** Same as SCSI-1, but uses a 50-pin connector instead of a 25-pin connector, and supports multiple devices. This is what most people mean when they refer to plain SCSI.

- Wide SCSI: Uses a wider cable (168 cable lines to 68 pins) to support 16-bit transfers.

- Fast SCSI: Uses an 8-bit bus, but doubles the clock rate to support data rates of 10 MBps.

- Fast Wide SCSI: Uses a 16-bit bus and supports data rates of 20 MBps.

- Ultra SCSI: Uses an 8-bit bus, and supports data rates of 20 MBps.

- SCSI-3: Uses a 16-bit bus and supports data rates of 40 MBps. Also called Ultra Wide SCSI.

- Ultra2 SCSI: Uses an 8-bit bus and supports data rates of 40 MBps.

- Wide Ultra2 SCSI: Uses a 16-bit bus and supports data rates of 80 MBps.

As the SCSI architecture has evolved over the last several years, especially with the advent of SCSI-3, the definition of SCSI has become misleading. As with any current standard, SCSI has evolved over time to:

- Keep pace with the ever-increasing options available for computers.

- Keep up with the increasing demands for performance and stability that are now expected not only of servers, but also from home PCs and higher-end workstations.

The most important fact to grasp is that SCSI provides a method for allowing access to multiple devices on the same "chain" or interface at the same time. Therefore, you should think of SCSI as a bus technology. The name says it all: Small Computer Systems Interface. One device on a SCSI bus (say, a Computer) can communicate directly to another (say, a disk drive) without going through the PCI bus, your system's DMA controller, or anything else aside from the SCSI controller. On thing to note, however, is that only one device can talk to one other device at a time over the bus. There is a large command set that melds the multiple SCSI implementations together and forms their foundation. As of SCSI-3, these commands are grouped under the following designations:

- The SCSI Block Commands (SBC) (Hard Disk Interface Commands.) In essence, these commands are designed for working with devices that access data in a non-sequential way. There is also a "reduced" subset of commands related to this (RBC).

- SCSI Stream Commands for tape drives (SSC). As opposed to SBC, this command set works with sequential data devices.

- SCSI Controller Commands for RAID arrays (SCC).

- Multimedia Commands (MMC) for devices such as DVD drives.

- SCSI Graphics Commands for printers (SGC).

- Media Changer Commands (SMC) for hardware such as CD-ROM jukeboxes.

- Enclosure Services Commands (SES)

- Object-based Storage Device (OSD)

- Management Server Commands (MSC)

Depending on implementation, the command groups may vary in definition and grouping, but the essentials remain the same. SCSI-3, now more commonly called ANSI SCSI, is what now constitutes the "SCSI" definition (and the command set listed above). Note that for a number of commands sets listed above, second generation proposals are now in the works. Such proposals, such as SBC-2, will be backwards compatible.

The commands (above) all fall under the mantle of "SCSI Block Commands" (SBC). The SCSI Primary Commands (SPC) set sits over these more base commands, providing the basis for SCSI interoperability--therefore, per the SCSI-3 specification, all SCSI devices must support SPC, otherwise the dream of true interoperability is not possible. Together, these two "units" serve as the command base for all SCSI controller hardware. With the introduction of Fibre Channel and SCSI-3, the protocol layer has been forced to branch into several directions. It is the job of the SCSI controller to handle the appropriate protocol path-- SCSI Interlocked Protocol serving the more common, SCSI Parallel interface, and SCSI Fibre Channel Protocol handling Fibre Channel requests. Prior to SCSI-3, the protocol would have tied directly to the SCSI Parallel Interface. This is illustrated in Figure 2.2.

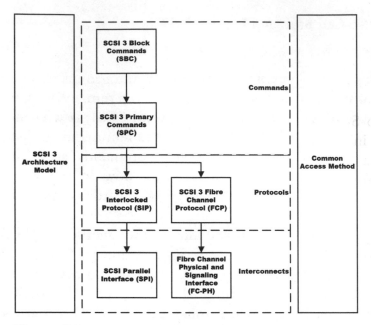

Figure 2.2: *SCSI Architecture*

SCSI 3 is the latest commonly available implementation of SCSI, let's examine it in more detail.

SCSI 3

In SCSI3 as with all SCSI, communication on the SCSI Bus is allowed between only two SCSI devices at a time. Some SCSI drives support systems with a maximum of eight SCSI devices including the host computer(s) connected to the SCSI bus. Other SCSI drives support systems with a maximum of sixteen SCSI devices on the SCSI bus.

Each SCSI device has a SCSI ID Bit assigned. The SCSI ID is assigned on some older drives by installing from 0 to 3 (8 device systems) jumper plugs or 0-4 (16 device systems) jumper plugs onto a connector in a binary coded configuration during system configuration. Some drive models have an interface that includes the SCSI bus ID lines, so that the host can set the drive ID over the interface. Drives that support SCAM protocol (SCSI Configured Automatically) can also have their drive ID assigned via interface.

When two SCSI devices communicate on the SCSI Bus, one acts as an initiator and the other acts as a target. The initiator (typically a host computer) originates an operation and the target performs the operation. The drive always operates as a target.

The Host Adapter/Initiator must be identified by one of the eight (or sixteen) SCSI Device Addresses. Make sure that none of the devices on the SCSI bus has duplicate addresses.

Specific SCSI bus functions are assigned to the initiator and other specific SCSI bus functions are assigned to the target. The initiator will select a particular target. The target will request the transfer of Command, Data, Status or other information on the data bus.

All transfers on the data bus are interlocked and follow a defined REQ/ACK Handshake protocol. One byte of information will be transferred with each handshake. However, synchronous data transfers do not require a one-for-one interlocking of REQ/ACK signals, but the total number of REQ pulses in a particular data transfer event must equal the total number of ACK pulses.

In general, SCSI drives support single initiator, single target; single initiator, multiple target; multiple initiator, single target; or multiple initiator, multiple target bus configurations.

SCSI drives respond to 8 distinct bus phases. The SCSI bus can never be in more than one phase at a time. The phases are:

- Bus Free phase -- The Bus Free phase indicates that no SCSI device is actively using the SCSI bus and it is available for subsequent users. In some cases, a target reverts to the Bus Free phase to indicate an error condition that it has no other way to handle. This is called an unexpected disconnect.

- Arbitration phase -- The Arbitration phase allows one SCSI device to gain control of the SCSI bus so that it can assume the role of an initiator or target.

- Selection phase -- The Selection phase allows an initiator to select a target for the purpose of initiating some target function (e.g., Read or Write command).

Note. During the Selection phase, the I/O signal is negated so this phase can be distinguished from the Reselection phase.

- Reselection phase -- Reselection is a phase that allows a target to reconnect to an initiator for the purpose of continuing some operation that was previously started by the initiator but was suspended by the target (i.e., the target disconnected by allowing a Bus Free phase to occur before the operation was complete). Reselection can be used only in systems that have Arbitration phase implemented. A SCSI drive implements the Reselection phase if the system is capable of supporting Reselection.

The following phases are collectively termed the Information transfer phases.

- Command phase -- The Command phase allows the target to request command information from the initiator.

- Data (in and out) -- The Data phase is a term that encompasses both the Data In phase and the Data Out phase.

  - Data In -- The Data In phase allows the target to request that it send data to the initiator. The target shall assert the I/O signal and negate the C/D and MSG signals during the REQ/ACK handshake(s) of this phase.

  - Data Out -- The Data Out phase allows the target to request that data be sent to it from the initiator. The target shall negate the C/D, I/O, and MSG signals during the REQ/ACK handshake(s) of this phase.

- Status (in only) -- The Status phase allows the target to request that it send status information to the initiator.

- Message (in and out) -- The Message phase is a term that references either a Message In or a Message Out phase. Multiple messages may be sent during either phase. Multiple byte messages shall be wholly contained with a single message phase.

  - Message In -- The Message In phase allows the target to request that it send message(s) to the initiator. The target shall assert C/D, I/O, and MSG during the REQ/ACK handshake(s) of this phase.

  - Message Out -- The Message Out phase allows the target to request that message(s) be sent from the initiator to the target. The target may invoke this phase at its convenience in response to the Attention condition created by the initiator. The target shall assert C/D and MSG and negate I/O during the REQ/ACK handshake(s) of this phase. The target shall handshake byte(s) in this phase until ATN goes false, unless an error occurs.

These phases are used to signal and communicate with the various devices on the SCSI bus. Figure 2-3 shows the phase flow diagrams for SCSI with and without the arbitration phase.

The arbitration phase is used depending on the type of devices and addressing used. For systems in which the Arbitration phase is implemented, the allowable sequences are shown in Figure 2.3.

The normal phase progression is from the Bus Free phase to Arbitration, from Arbitration to Selection or Reselection, and from Selection or Reselection to one or more of the information transfer phases (Command, Data, Status, or Message).

There are no restrictions on the sequences between information transfer phases. A phase type may even be followed by the same phase type (e.g., a Data phase may be followed by another Data phase). However, a Data phase must follow a command phase except after a reselection phase.

SCSI is rapidly becoming the standard interface for all small and mid-ranged computer disk farms.

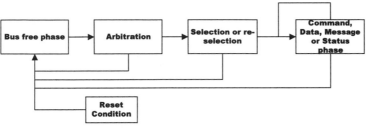

Phase flow with arbitration

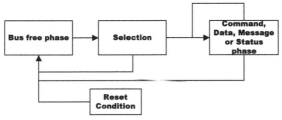

Phase flow without arbitration

Figure 2.3: *Comparison of SCSI Phase Flows*

Of course, each of the SCSI phases has discrete timing intervals that it follows in order to allow the orderly transfer of messages between two devices. Table 2.2 shows the specified timing limits for the SCSI 3 implementation of the interface.

PARAMETER	DELAY	DESCRIPTION
Arbitration delay	2.4 µs	The minimum time a SCSI device shall wait from asserting BSY for arbitration until the Data Bus can be examined to see if arbitration has been won. There is no maximum time.

PARAMETER	DELAY	DESCRIPTION
Assertion period	90 ns	The minimum time that a target shall assert REQ while using synchronous data transfers. Also, the minimum time that an initiator shall assert ACK while using synchronous data transfers.
Bus clear delay	800 ns	The maximum time for a SCSI device to stop driving all bus signals after: 1. The Bus Free phase is detected (BSY and SEL both negated for a bus settle delay). 2. SEL is received from another SCSI device during the Arbitration phase. 3. The transition of RST to assertion. Note. For the first condition above, the maximum time for a SCSI device to clear the bus is 1200 ns from BSY and SEL first becoming both negated. If a SCSI device requires more than a bus settle delay to detect Bus Free phase, it shall clear the bus within a Bus Clear delay minus the excess time.

PARAMETER	DELAY	DESCRIPTION
Bus free delay	800 ns	The minimum time that a SCSI device shall wait from its detection of the Bus Free phase (BSY and SEL both negated for a bus settle delay) until its assertion of BSY when going to the Arbitration phase.
Bus set delay	1.8 µs	The maximum time for a SCSI device to assert BSY and its SCSI ID bit on the Data Bus after it detects Bus Free phase (BSY and SEL both negated for a bus settle delay) for the purpose of entering the Arbitration phase.
Bus settle delay	400 ns	The time to wait for the bus to settle after changing certain control signals as specified in the protocol definitions.
Cable skew delay	10 ns	The maximum difference in propagation time allowed between any two SCSI bus signals when measured between any two SCSI devices.
Data release delay	400 ns	The maximum time for an initiator to release the Data Bus signals following the transition of the I/O signal from negation to assertion.

PARAMETER	DELAY	DESCRIPTION
Deskew delay	45 ns	The minimum time required for deskew of certain signals.
Disconnection delay	200 µs	The minimum time that a target shall wait after releasing BSY before participating in an Arbitration phase when honoring a Disconnect message from the initiator.
Hold time	45 ns	The minimum time added between the assertion of REQ or ACK and the changing of the data lines to provide hold time in the initiator or target, respectively, while using synchronous data transfers. The minimum time that a target shall negate REQ while using synchronous data transfers. Also, the minimum time that an initiator shall negate ACK while using synchronous data transfers.
Reset hold time	25 µs	The minimum time for which RST is asserted. There is no maximum time.

PARAMETER	DELAY	DESCRIPTION
Selection abort time	200 µs	The maximum time that a target (or initiator) shall take from its most recent detection of being selected (or reselected) until asserting a BSY response. This timeout is required to ensure that a target (or initiator) does not assert BSY after a Selection (or Reselection) phase has been aborted. This is not the selection timeout period.
Selection timeout delay	250 ms	The minimum time an initiator (or target) should wait for a BSY response during the Selection (or Reselection) phase before starting the timeout procedure. The drive implements this 250 ms selection timeout delay.
Transfer period	negotiated	The minimum time allowed between the leading edges of successive REQ pulses and of successive ACK pulses while using synchronous data transfers.

Table 2.2 *SCSI Timing Limits*

Fast synchronous transfer option -- When SCSI devices negotiate a synchronous data transfer period of less than 200 ns, they are said to be using "fast synchronous data transfers."

Devices, which negotiate a synchronous data transfer period □ 200 ns, use timing parameters specified in Table 2.2. When a fast synchronous data transfer period is negotiated, those specific times redefined in Table 2.3 are used; those not redefined remain the same. The minimum allowed synchronous data transfer period is 100 ns.

PARAMETER	TIMING	DESCRIPTION
Fast assertion period	30 ns	This value is the minimum time that a target shall assert REQ while using fast synchronous data transfers. Also, the minimum time that an initiator shall assert ACK while using fast synchronous data transfers.
Fast cable skew delay	5 ns	This value is the maximum difference in propagation time allowed between any two SCSI bus signals measured between any two SCSI devices while using fast synchronous data transfers.
Fast deskew delay	20 ns	This value is the minimum time required for deskew of certain signals while using fast synchronous data transfers.
Fast hold time	10 ns	This value is the minimum time added between the assertion of REQ or ACK and the changing of the data lines to provide hold time in the initiator or target respectively, while using fast synchronous data transfers.

PARAMETER	TIMING	DESCRIPTION
Fast negation period	30 ns	This value is the minimum time that a target shall negate REQ while using fast synchronous data transfers. Also, the minimum time that an initiator shall negate ACK while using fast synchronous data transfers.

Table 2.3: *SCSI 3 Fast Transfer Timing Limits*

In the chapters on arrays and tuning, we will see where understanding the various limits and phases in the SCSI interface are important.

Next, we will examine the IEEE1394 Interface.

IEEE1394 Interface

IEEE1394 is the standard designation for a very fast external bus standard that supports data transfer rates of up to 400Mbps (in 1394a) and 800Mbps over copper (in 1394b). Products supporting the 1394 standard go under different names, depending on the company that has developed them. Apple, which originally developed the technology, uses the trademarked name FireWire (many companies refuse to pay Apple for the right to use the Firewire name so they use other names, such as *i.link* and *Lynx*, to describe their 1394 products.)

In the current standard a single 1394 port can be used to connect up 63 external chained devices (Compare this to IDE's 2 and SCSI's 16 device maximums.) In addition to its high speed, 1394 also supports isochronous data (defined as the capability to deliver data at a guaranteed rate.) This makes it ideal for devices that need to transfer high levels of data in real-time, such as video devices.

While more expensive than IDE Disks, IEE1394 disks are generally less expensive than SCSI based disks.

IEEE-1394 is defined as part of the SCSI-3 family of related standards, and was at one point called "serial SCSI". It is, in fact, a type of SCSI, based on the broad coverage of SCSI-3, which goes beyond regular SCSI to cover several similar, "SCSI-like" technologies. In terms of signaling and some aspects of operation, IEEE-1394 actually can be thought of as "serial SCSI".

In terms of configuration and how it is used in the PC, IEEE-1394 is better thought of as "USB, only faster". It is a serial interface that supports hot swapping, and plug-and-play. IEEE-1394 supports up to 400 Mbits/second (or greater.) When originally introduced, IEEE-1394 had considerable promise, and there were some analysts who thought it would eventually become a major player in the mainstream hard disk interface market. For example, while it is not as fast as high-speed implementations of SCSI, it is considerably simpler to implement, and doesn't suffer from the speed limitations of USB.

In spite of its strengths, IEEE-1394 has not been heavily utilized as a storage interface within the PC. There could be any number of reasons for this, maybe its Apple origins have stifled its use in PCs, IEEE-1394 is not a major player in the storage industry. Some newer systems are now equipped with this interface, and a variety of storage devices are made for it, so it is a viable option if your system supports it, or if you wish to add support for it there are commercially available PCI compatible interface cards.

The IEEE 1394 standard defines both a backplane physical layer and a point-to-point cable-connected virtual bus implementations. The backplane version operates at 12.5, 25 or 50 Mbits/sec. The cable version supports data rates of 100, 200 and 400 Mbits/ sec. Both versions are compatible at the link layer and above. The Standard defines the media, topology, and the protocol.

IEEE 1394 is:

- A digital interface - no need to convert digital data into analog for better signal integrity

- A physically small thin serial cable - replaces today's bulky and expensive interfaces

- Easy to use - no need for terminators, device IDs, screws, or complicated set-ups

- Hot pluggable - devices can be added and removed while the bus is active

- Scalable - the Standard defines 100, 200, and 400 Mbps devices and can support the multiple speeds on a single bus

- Flexible - the Standard supports freeform daisy chaining and branching for peer-to-peer implementations

- Fast, guaranteed bandwidth - the Standard supports guaranteed delivery of time critical data which enables smaller buffers (lower cost)

As mentioned above, IEEE1394 supports two types of data transfer: asynchronous and isochronous. For traditional computer memory-mapped, load and store applications, asynchronous transfer is appropriate and adequate. One of IEEE1394's key features is its support of isochronous data channels. Isochronous data transfer provides guaranteed data transport at a pre-determined rate. This is critical for multimedia applications where uninterrupted transport of time-critical data and just-in-time delivery reduce the need for costly buffering. This leads to perhaps one of the most important uses of IEEE1394 as the digital interface for consumer electronics and AV peripherals.

IEEE1394, like SCSI, is a peer-to-peer interface. This allows, for example, dubbing from one camcorder to another without a computer. It also allows multiple computers to share a given peripheral without any special support in the peripheral or the computers. It is a result of all of these features that IEEE1394 has become the digital interface of choice and its acceptance is growing.

IEEE1394a, in its peer-to-peer bus topology, allows 100 to 400 Mbps data transfer rates for up to 63 nodes, allowing16 hops 4.5 at meters per hop. IEEE1394 also allows for Isochronous and asynchronous data transfer A/V, storage, printing, scanning, TCP/IP networking.

IEEE1394b allows for higher speeds and longer distances. IEEE1394b is completely compatible with IEEE 1394a, providing up to 800 Mbps to 3200 Mbps data transfer over 4.5 meters copper and 100 Mbps over 100 meter copper. If used with Category 5 UTP wiring, you get 400 Mbps over 100 meter plastic optical fiber. You get 3200 Mbps over 100 meters of glass optical fiber. Each standard copper 1394 bus can have a maximum 72 m of cables with no more than 4.5 m between each device/node. (Bridges can expand this network.) Virtually any device can be connected (drives, camcorders, UPS, lights, etc.).

The IEEE1394 bus automatically initializes itself when it is powered on and whenever a device/node is added or removed. A half-duplex packet bus, 1394 automatically arbitrates between asynchronous and isochronous (time-dependent) transmissions, setting fair intervals, so that all devices waiting to send data get a chance to do so. Interface boards with IEEE1394 interfaces are compatible with PCI-bus

IEEE1394 protocol Layers

The IEEE1394 interface is a three-layer protocol stack. The three layers include:

- Transaction Layer -- Implements the request/response protocol.

- Link Layer -- responsible for getting data on and off the cable, error detection and correction, retransmission, cycle control for isosynchronous transfer, supply of the awk datagram to the transaction layer.

- Physical Layer -- provides initialization and arbitration services. This layer provides for electrical signaling, mechanical connectors and cabling, the arbitration mechanisms, the serial coding and decoding, and transfer speed detection.

These layers are sandwiched between the Serial API above the transactional layer and the IEEE 1394 physical interface below the physical layer. The three layers and the serial API communicate to the computers serial bus interface. This architecture for the IEEE1394 interface is shown in Figure 2.4.

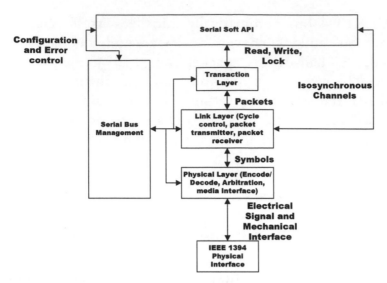

Figure 2.4: *IEEE1394 Protocol Stack*

As with the SCSI bus, only one pair of devices at a time can communicate over the IEEE1394 bus.

To conclude the discussion of disk interfaces, we'll look at the fibre channel interface.

Fibre Channel

The term "Fibre Channel" is used to designate an American National Standards Institute (ANSI) interface that acts as a general transport vehicle to simultaneously deliver the command sets of several existing interface protocols including SCSI-3, IPI-3, HIPPI-FP, IP, and ATM/AAL5. This doesn't mean that proprietary and other command sets may not also use and share the Fibre Channel, but these are not yet defined as part of the Fibre Channel standard. In this chapter, we will discuss Fibre Channel Arbitrated Loop (FC-AL) as one topology used to connect two or more devices within the guidelines set by the ANSI standards.

Fibre Channel is designed to support both the transfer of large and small data sets. This allows it to be efficient in the transfer of a wide variety of data and, therefore, it can be used in systems ranging from supercomputers to individual workstations. Fibre Channel peripherals can include devices such as, but not limited to, disk drives, tape units, high-bandwidth graphics terminals, and laser printers. For our purpose, we are concerned with disk drives

In order to accommodate all of these device types with various command sets, Fibre Channel separates the physical I/O interface from the I/O operations. This allows the use of multiple command sets simultaneously. This separation of the physical IO interface from the IO operations allows new speeds and new functions to be added without negating all previous investment in existing components, connectors and cables.

Another advantage of Fibre Channel is that it supports both channel and network peripheral protocols for device communication. This means that channel and network protocols can share the same physical medium.

Fibre Channel was designed to not have its own native I/O command set protocol. It allows other protocols to superimpose their command sets onto itself and then simply transports this information. However, Fibre Channel does have a command set that it uses to manage the links between the various participating devices using Fibre Channel "link services."

Since multiple command sets may use Fibre Channel, it identifies the information by command set type. This is accomplished by each Fibre Channel frame having a field in the frame header that identifies the protocol associated with that frame, this allows the receiving port to distinguish among the protocols and make the proper processing decisions.

As mentioned above, Fibre Channel supports both channel and network communications. Let's look at this.

Channels and Fibre Channel

Traditional disk drive communications occur in a channel environment where the host controls the devices attached to it. The primary requirement for channel environments is to provide error-free delivery, at the bit level, with transfer delays being a secondary consideration.

Networks and Fibre Channel

Networks are designed to allow many devices to communicate with each other as desired. This usually involves software support to route transactions to the correct provider and to verify access permission. Networks are generally used for transferring data with "error-free delivery" and voice and video where "delivery on time" is the primary requirement with error-free delivery being a secondary consideration. For example, when transferring video, it is more important to provide on-time delivery of data to prevent loss of video frames than to lose one or two pixels in a video frame.

Fibre Topologies

The term topologies include all the elements necessary to successfully connect two or more nodes (also known as devices). There are several topologies available with Fibre Channel, but all of them have common components: nodes, ports, and links.

The ANSI Fibre Channel standard defines three topologies:

- Arbitrated loop (Fibre Channel Arbitrated Loop, FC-AL)
- Fabric
- Point-to-point

Note. Some brief discussions about items not directly associated with arbitrated loop and fabric topologies are included to make you aware that other topologies exist within the constructs of the ANSI Fibre Channel standard.

The fabric topology permits dynamic interconnections between nodes through ports connected to a fabric. This fabric is similar to a switch or router and is often compared to a telephone system because of its redundant rerouting capabilities. The fabric topology also allows multiple connections simultaneously, unlike FC-AL, which results in a single circuit being established between only two ports at any one particular time. Fabric and arbitrated loop topologies may be combined in one system to provide a wide variety of services and performance levels to the nodes.

Point-to-point topologies are used only to connect two ports without any routing capabilities.

Nodes

All Fibre Channel devices are called nodes. This is a generic term describing any device (workstation, printer, disk drive, scanner, etc.) connected to a Fibre Channel topology. Each node has at least one port, called an N_Port to provide access to other nodes. The "N" in N_Port stands for node. As you will see later, ports used in a Fibre Channel Arbitrated Loop topology are called NL_Ports where the "NL" stands for node loop.

The components that connect two or more node ports together are what are collectively called a topology. Nodes work within the provided topology to communicate with all other nodes.

Ports

Ports provide the link to the outside world for a Fibre Channel node. As stated above, each node has at least one port (usually 2) to provide access to other nodes. Most manufacturers' fibre channel drives have two ports. Each port utilizes a pair of fibers, one to carry information into the port and one to carry information out of the port. This pair of fibers (sometimes they are actually copper wire) is called a "link" and is part of each topology. The Fibre Channel ANSI specification also supports fibers made of optical strands as a medium for data transfer.

As stated above, ports used in a FC-AL topology are called node loop ports (NL_Ports). In addition to NL_Ports, other port types exist as shown in Table 2.4.

PORT TYPE	LOCATION	ASSOCIATED TOPOLOGY
N_Port	Node	Point-to-point or Fabric
NL_Port	Node	in N_Port mode—Point-to-point or Fabric, in NL_Port mode—Arbitrated Loop
F_Port	Fabric	Fabric
FL_Port	Fabric	in F_Port mode—Fabric, in FL_Port mode—Arbitrated Loop
E_Port	Fabric	Internal Fabric Expansion
G_Port	Fabric	in F_Port mode—Fabric, in E_Port mode—Internal fabric expansion

PORT TYPE	LOCATION	ASSOCIATED TOPOLOGY
GL_Port	Fabric	in F_Port mode—Fabric, in FL_Port mode—Arbitrated Loop' in E_Port mode—Internal fabric expansion

Table 2.4: *Fibre Channel Port Types*

Fibre Channel Links

Each port is comprised of two fibers, the one that carries the information into the port is called a receiver. The one that carries information out of the port and is called a transmitter. The Fibre Channel standard supports two types of fibers— electrical wires (most commonly copper) and optical strands. This pair of fibres or wires is what we call a link.

The purpose of the links is to carry the data frames between the nodes. Each link in a Fibre Channel topology can handle multiple frame types; this allows frame multiplexing. For example, a frame containing TCP/IP information may be followed by a frame containing SCSI, followed by a frame containing some other protocol's information.

Arbitrated Loop Topology

Fibre Channel Arbitrated Loops (FC-AL) use a loop structure to attach multiple nodes without the use of hubs and switches. Arbitration is used by the node ports to establish a point-to-point circuit. FC-AL is a distributed topology where each L_Port includes the minimum necessary function to establish the circuit. From two to 126 node ports can be connected using the arbitrated loop topology. Figure 2.5 shows a four-node arbitrated loop setup.

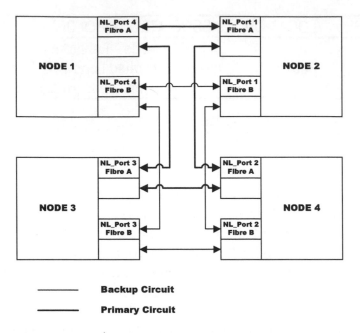

NL_Port 4 Fibre A / NL_Port 1 Fibre A

NODE 1 / NODE 2

NL_Port 4 Fibre B / NL_Port 1 Fibre B

NL_Port 3 Fibre A / NL_Port 2 Fibre A

NODE 3 / NODE 4

NL_Port 3 Fibre B / NL_Port 2 Fibre B

—— Backup Circuit

—— Primary Circuit

Figure 2.5: *Four-Node Arbitrated Loop Set Up*

In an arbitrated loop topology, the ports are called NL_Ports (Node Loop Ports). Each of the NL_Ports has an input and output connection. The actual ports are located on the host's backpanel, not on the disk drive. Dual ports are usually provided for redundancy so that if one loop fails, the other one can fulfill the loop duties. Each disk drive usually has one Fibre Channel single connector attachment (SCA) connector.

The arbitrated loop protocol is known as a token acquisition protocol. This means each port on the same arbitrated loop sees all messages, but only takes messages that are addressed to it, passing along all others.

When energized, each NL_Port signs in with the other ports on its loop. The NL_Port will first attempt to locate an FL_Port. If the NL_Port finds an FL_Port, it knows it is attached to a public loop connected to a fabric. If the port does not locate an FL_Port, it then knows it is a part of a private loop with other NL_Ports only.

There can be up to 126 active NL_Ports and up to one active FL_Port attached to the same arbitrated loop. If, for some reason, an NL_Port does not attempt to discover an FL_Port and there is an FL_Port present, the NL_Port is only allowed to access other NL_Ports on the same loop.

Ports are usually equipped with port bypass circuitry that allows the port to be bypassed when it is malfunctioning or a device in a loop has been removed. These are known as PBCs and are generally located external to the drives or devices.

To provide an analogy, a SCSI chain is like a neighborhood, the fibre channel acts as the highway connecting multiple neighborhoods.

Now that we have looked at the various disk interface technologies, we will look at some basic ways to optimize them in the next chapter.

Conclusion

There are three basic technologies for disk interfaces, ATA, which is suitable for small desk top systems requiring little IO bandwidth and only a few drive (usually less than 4), SCSI, which is the de facto standard disk interface for almost all production servers due to its relatively high bandwidth and flexibility, and IEEE1394, which shows a lot of promise but hasn't really caught on yet in the server market. In addition to those, we have the fibre channel technology, which can be used to tie multiple SCSI disk chains together and offers large bandwidth.

References

IEEE1394 Firewire/ilink, XILINX, ESP - Emerging Standards and Protocols, PowerPoint Presentation, www.xilinx.com

Information Technology -AT Attachment with Packet Interface - 5 (ATA/ATAPI-5), Working Draft T13 1321D, Revision 3, 29 February 2000, Reference number ANSI NCITS.*** - xxxx, Printed February, 29, 2000 10:06AM

Seagate Fibre Channel Interface Product Manual, 1997, 1998, 1999, 2000 Seagate Technology, LLC, All rights reserved
August 2000, Publication number: 77767496, Rev. B

Seagate SCSI Interface Product Manual, Volume 2, 1997-1999 Seagate Technology, Inc. All rights reserved, Publication number: 77738479, Rev. J, April 1999

Optimizing Disk Performance

Optimizing Your Disk Interface

Each of the disk interfaces we have discussed in Chapter 2 is optimized in a different manner. In some cases, there may be little or nothing you can do to adjust how the interface is used by your system, in others, you may have almost complete control. For example, the ATA interface can be adjusted in Linux using the *hdparm* command. While in Windows, you may have little or no ability to adjust the ATA interface. Let's begin with the ATA interface.

Now...let's talk about optimizing performance...

Optimizing ATA Performance

Generally speaking, if you are dealing with ATA disks you will be using a Windows2000 server or a Linux server. You will probably have a maximum of 4 internal IDE/ATA drives with the operating system and software occupying one of the drives. Hopefully, the swap area will be spread over several drives, as will the database (unless the ATA drives have been RAIDed).

In Windows2000 and Linux, you should be sure the latest firmware for your controller has been downloaded and flashed onto your controller chips. If you have a drive card, make sure it is the latest technology.

ATA Tuning In Windows

Other than getting the best drivers, the best interface cards and the fastest disks, there isn't much else in Windows to be done at the interface level. However, there are a few things to improve EIDE performance:

- Enable DMA for the operating system, for Windows 2000 this is done by:

  1. Right click on *My Computer* and choose *Manage*

  2. Click on Device Manager

  3. Click on the (+) sign next to *IDE ATA/ATAPI controllers*

  4. Double click on the controller you want to change/check

  5. Click on Advanced Settings

  6. Select the drop-down menu for Transfer Mode and make sure *DMA if available* is selected.

7. Below the drop-down, you will see *Current Transfer Mode*. This should display Ultra DMA Mode 2, 4 or 5 depending on your system.

If *DMA if available* is already set, but the transfer mode shows PIO, toggle the setting by selecting *PIO Only* and click OK, then repeat the above steps.

- Enable IDE Block Mode in the system BIOS. This will allow the system to do multiple read/write operations simultaneously to improve throughput. This will probably involve reboot and then using the system specific keystrokes to enable your BIOS editor. This can be called Block Mode, IDE Block Mode or Multi-Sector Transfer. The settings for this range are from 0 to 32 sectors. You need to verify that your drive will support this mode. In a single read/write operation, the higher the settings the more blocks transferred, thereby reducing the load on the system.

- Make sure hard drives are not slaves to CD-ROMS or other ATA-EIDE devices. Hard drives should always be the masters on an EIDE chain (usually the last drive in the chain is the master with cable-select).

- Make sure the fastest hard drive is set as the master drive in an EIDE chain.

- Adding additional RAM will reduce the systems dependence on drive space for virtual memory, thus improving throughput.

At the physical disk level in Windows, you should implement a defragmentation routine to make sure your drives are not fragmented. Fragmentation in Windows is endemic to the operating system and will occur, robbing you of up to 70% of your disk performance. In one test, boot time went from over 15 minutes to less than 5 when the server's disks were defragmented. Performance improvements of a similar nature can be expected from your Oracle system if it is located on ATA drives in Windows as well.

Figure 3.1 shows a screen capture from a seldom-used Windows 2000 system drive (all data and file storage is done to a shared file system). Notice even a lightly used drive is showing over 20% fragmentation. On a laptop using NT4.0 SP6a, after two years of work, the drive was 100% fragmented! No wonder performance was terrible.

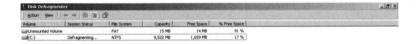

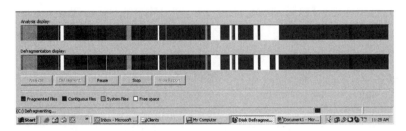

Figure 3.1: *Disk Fragmentation on Windows*

Figure 3.2 shows the report that goes along with the display in Figure 3.1.

```
Volume (C:):
    Volume size                          = 9,522 MB
    Cluster size                         = 512 bytes
    Used space                           = 7,862 MB
    Free space                           = 1,659 MB
    Percent free space                   = 17 %
```

```
Volume fragmentation
      Total fragmentation                    = 27 %
      File fragmentation                     = 54 %
      Free space fragmentation               = 0 %

File fragmentation
      Total files                            = 86,076
      Average file size                      = 113 KB
      Total fragmented files                 = 2,252
      Total excess fragments                 = 51,322
      Average fragments per file             = 1.59

Pagefile fragmentation
      Pagefile size                          = 384 MB
      Total fragments                        = 4

Directory fragmentation
      Total directories                      = 9,736
      Fragmented directories                 = 645
      Excess directory fragments             = 4,222

Master File Table (MFT) fragmentation
      Total MFT size                         = 130 MB
      MFT record count                       = 96,071
      Percent MFT in use                     = 71 %
      Total MFT fragments                    = 3

----------------------------------------------------------------
Fragments      File Size       Most fragmented files
199            820 KB
\oracle\ora9i\oem_webstage\sysman\reporting\webhelp\dba
213            1,595 KB        \Documents and Settings\AULTM\Local
Settings\TEMP\Going out for the LOB2.doc
155            143 KB          \Documents and Settings\AULTM\Local
Settings\TEMP\VBE\MSForms.exd
428            5,125 KB        \Documents and Settings\All
Users\Application Data\Symantec\Norton AntiVirus Corporate
Edition\7.5\vd173c10.vdb
131            2,000 KB        \Documents and Settings\AULTM\Local
Settings\TEMP\Acr18F.tmp
109            468 KB
\oracle\ora9i\oem_webstage\oracle\sysman\resources
188            816 KB
\oracle\ora9i\oem_webstage\oracle\sysman\help\master\dba
119            9,511 KB        \oracle\ora9i\oem_webstage\java-
plugin\jinit11818.exe
201            162 KB          \Documents and Settings\AULTM\Local
Settings\TEMP\Word8.0\MSForms.exd
431            5,100 KB        \Documents and Settings\All
Users\Application Data\Symantec\Norton AntiVirus Corporate
Edition\7.5\xfer_tmp\3FE8FACA.xfr
129            5,042 KB        \Program
Files\Oracle\Inventory\logs\installActions2001-10-12_02-00-45-PM.log
342            16,739 KB
\oracle\ora9i\ldap\oidadmin\osdadminhelp.jar
203            11,036 KB       \oracle\ora9i\jlib\cvd.zip
```

```
495           44,437 KB          \oracle\ora9i\jlib\oembase-9_2_0.jar
125            4,828 KB          \oracle\ora9i\jlib\oemlt-9_2_0.jar
139            1,013 KB          \WINNT\SECURITY\LOGS\winlogon.log
293            5,100 KB          \Documents and Settings\All
Users\Application Data\Symantec\Norton AntiVirus Corporate
Edition\7.5\VD172E09.VDB
415            4,955 KB          \Documents and Settings\All
Users\Application Data\Symantec\Norton AntiVirus Corporate
Edition\7.5\xfer_tmp\3F8DD5E8.xfr
169              85 KB          \WINNT\DirectX.log
204             820 KB          \oracle\ora9i\doc\EM\Webhelp\dba
237            2,980 KB          \oracle\ora9i\dm\doc\odmjdoc.tar
1,118         54,880 KB
\oracle\ora9i\demo\schema\sales_history\sh_sales.dat
138           22,881 KB
\oracle\ora9i\ctx\data\frlx\droldF.dat
255           36,881 KB
\oracle\ora9i\ctx\data\enlx\droldUS.dat
155           28,784 KB          \oracle\ora9i\BIN\oracle.exe
2,700          156 MB
\oracle\ora9i\assistants\dbca\templates\Data_Warehouse.dfj
955            143 MB
\oracle\ora9i\assistants\dbca\templates\Transaction_Processing.dfj
192            203 KB
\oracle\ora9i\admin\OEMREP\bdump\alert_oemrep.log
223            238 KB
\oracle\ora9i\admin\aultdb2\bdump\alert_aultdb2.log
1,777         53,148 KB          \Documents and Settings\AULTM\Local
Settings\Temporary Internet
Files\Content.IE5\NCGWIBWI\10i_beta1_lnx_Disk1.cpio[1].gz
```

Figure 3.2: *Example Windows 2000 Fragmentation Report*

In order to fix the above fragmentation, it took multiple passes through the defragmentation routine provided by Windows2000. The first pass resulted in extreme freespace fragmentation, which would have caused the first file that was written after defragmentation to be fragmented! After 5 passes, the fragmentation was down to 12%, after 9 passes, 10%, which seemed to be the best it could do, leaving 21% of the files fragmented. Figure 3.3 shows the final screen shot after optimization.

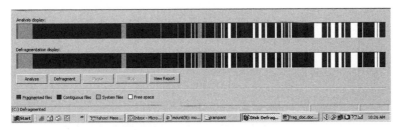

Figure 3.3: *Final Defragmentation Screen*

The final report from the defragmentation utility is shown in Figure 3.4. Compare the initial report with the final report and you can see significant reduction in the number of fragments, especially in the directories and system files.

```
Volume (C:):
    Volume size                     = 9,522 MB
    Cluster size                    = 512 bytes
    Used space                      = 7,890 MB
    Free space                      = 1,632 MB
    Percent free space              = 17 %

Volume fragmentation
    Total fragmentation             = 10 %
    File fragmentation              = 21 %
    Free space fragmentation        = 0 %

File fragmentation
    Total files                     = 86,252
    Average file size               = 113 KB
    Total fragmented files          = 24
    Total excess fragments          = 58
    Average fragments per file      = 1.00
```

```
Pagefile fragmentation
     Pagefile size                           = 384 MB
     Total fragments                         = 4

Directory fragmentation
     Total directories                       = 9,745
     Fragmented directories                  = 1
     Excess directory fragments              = 1

Master File Table (MFT) fragmentation
     Total MFT size                          = 130 MB
     MFT record count                        = 96,332
     Percent MFT in use                      = 71 %
     Total MFT fragments                     = 3


-----------------------------------------------------------------
Fragments       File Size       Files that did not defragment
9               1 KB            \WINNT\SYSTEM32\CONFIG\SOFTWARE.LOG
2               32 KB           \WINNT\SYSTEM32\CONFIG\SECURITY
2               1 KB            \WINNT\SYSTEM32\CONFIG\SECURITY.LOG
4               3,148 KB        \WINNT\SYSTEM32\CONFIG\SYSTEM
2               257 KB          \WINNT\SECURITY\LOGS\scepol.log
2               65 KB
\oracle\ora9i\oramts\trace\OracleMTSRecoveryService(664).trc
2               17 KB           \Documents and Settings\AULTM\Local
Settings\Temporary Internet
Files\Content.IE5\NCGWIBWI\mount.8[1].html
3               121 MB          \Documents and Settings\AULTM\Local
Settings\Application Data\Microsoft\Outlook\outlook.pst
2               10 KB           \Documents and Settings\AULTM\Local
Settings\TEMP\SOF2.tmp
8               1 KB            \Documents and
Settings\AULTM\NTUSER.DAT.LOG
2               10 KB           \Documents and Settings\AULTM\Local
Settings\TEMP\SOFF.tmp
2               3 KB            \Documents and Settings\AULTM\Local
Settings\TEMP\SOF10.tmp
2               3 KB            \Documents and Settings\AULTM\Local
Settings\TEMP\SOF11.tmp
5               330 MB          \Documents and Settings\AULTM\Local
Settings\Application Data\Microsoft\Outlook\archive.pst
2               145 MB
\oracle\ora9i\oradata\OEMREP\EXAMPLE01.DBF
4               330 MB
\oracle\ora9i\oradata\OEMREP\SYSTEM01.DBF
2               200 MB
\oracle\ora9i\oradata\OEMREP\UNDOTBS01.DBF
2               148 MB
\oracle\ora9i\oradata\aultdb2\EXAMPLE01.DBF
4               400 MB
\oracle\ora9i\oradata\aultdb2\SYSTEM01.DBF
2               25 KB
\oracle\ora9i\network\log\agntsrvc.log
2               64 KB           \oracle\ora9i\network\log\dbsnmp.log
2               1,187 KB
\oracle\ora9i\network\log\listener.log
```

```
2           156 MB
\oracle\ora9i\assistants\dbca\templates\Data_Warehouse.dfj
2           540 KB          \WINNT\ShellIconCache
```

Figure 3.4: *Final Fragmentation Report*

To reduce the chance of fragmentation in Windows with Oracle, consider using raw partitions (partitions where Oracle handles the IO to the disk instead of the operating system.) Windows uses an optimistic write algorithm that writes blocks back to the first available location, not their original location, causing Windows to fragment from day one of operation.

Some claim that since the file system in Windows (or AIX or VMS) is designed to fragment, it performs better when fragmented. This statement seems odd since every time you defragment in Windows (or AIX or VMS) your performance improves. If this old SA tale where true, wouldn't performance get worse when you defragment?

ATA Tuning in LINUX

You will be happy to know that LINUX is specifically designed (as are other true "UNIXs", SCO not included) to not fragment hard drives. Fragmentation is reduced in LINUX over Windows by usually more than 98 percent and is usually not a concern.

However, Linux takes any default drive interface settings where implemented by the developer of the ATA kernel module that interfaces to your EIDE/ATA disk drive. At the time the driver was written, no doubt the drives were inferior to what you are currently running, not to mention it may have been written with old interface drivers as well. Fear not! LINUX provides the *hdparm* utility to reset the values for the ATA interface to take advantage of new drives and better interfaces. Thus, if you want to tune the ATA drives in LINUX use *hdparm*. In some cases, the disk IO rate increased by nearly 500 percent (a factor of 5) over pre-tuned values by the proper application of the *hdparm* application parameters. The basic tuning related arguments for *hdparm* are:

When no flags are given, acdgkmnru is assumed.

- **-a** - Get/set sector count for file system read-ahead. This is used to improve performance in sequential reads of large files by pre-fetching additional blocks in anticipation of them being needed by the running task. In the current kernel version (2.0.10), this has a default setting of 8 sectors (4KB). This value seems good for most purposes, but in a system where most file accesses are random seeks, a smaller setting might provide better performance. In addition, many IDE drives have a separate built-in read-ahead function, which alleviates the need for a file system read-ahead in many situations.

- **-A** - Disable/enable the IDE drive's read-look ahead feature (usually ON by default).

- **-B** - Set Advanced Power Management feature, if the drive supports it. A low value means aggressive power management and a high value means better performance. A value of 255 will disable apm (automatic power management) on the drive. When a drive spins down due to reaching its apm timeout, it may take up to 30 seconds to respond to the first request after the timeout.

- **-c** - Query/enable (E)IDE 32-bit I/O support. A numeric parameter can be used to enable/disable 32-bit I/O support: Currently supported values include 0 to disable 32-bit I/O support (sets it to 16 bit), 1 to enable 32-bit data transfers, and 3 to enable 32-bit data transfers with a special sync sequence required by many chipsets. The value 3 works with nearly all 32-bit IDE chipsets, but incurs slightly more overhead. Note that "32-bit" refers to data transfers across a PCI or VLB bus to the interface card only; all (E)IDE drives still have a 16-bit connection over the ribbon cable from the interface card.

- **-d** - Disable/enable the "*using_dma*" flag for this drive. This option now works with most combinations of drives and PCI interfaces, which support DMA and which are known to the IDE driver. It is also a good idea to use the appropriate -X option in combination with -d1 to ensure the drive itself is programmed for the correct DMA mode, although most BIOSs should do this for you at boot time. Using DMA nearly always gives the best performance, with fast I/O throughput and low CPU usage. But there are at least a few configurations of chipsets and drives for which DMA does not make much of a difference, or may even slow things down (on really messed up hardware!). Your mileage may vary.

- **-f** - Sync and flush the buffer cache for the device on exit. This operation is also performed as part of the -t and -T timings.

- **-g** - Display the drive geometry (cylinders, heads, sectors), the size (in sectors) of the device, and the starting offset (in sectors) of the device from the beginning of the drive.

- **-i** - Display the identification info that was obtained from the drive at boot time, if available. This is a feature of modern IDE drives and may not be supported by older devices. The data returned may or may not be current, depending on activity since booting the system. However, the current multiple sector mode count is always shown. For a more detailed interpretation of the identification info, refer to ATA attachment Interface for Disk Drives

(ANSI ASC X3T9.2 working draft, revision 4a, April 19/93).

- **-I** - Request identification info directly from the drive, which is displayed in a new expanded format with considerably more detail than with the older -i flag. There is a special "no seatbelts" variation on this option, **-Istdin,** which cannot be combined with any other options, and which accepts a drive identification block as standard input instead of using a /dev/hd* parameter. The format of this block must be exactly the same as that found in the /proc/ide/*/hd*/identify "files". This variation is designed for use with "libraries" of drive identification information and can also be used on ATAPI drives, which may give media errors with the standard mechanism.

- **-k** - Get/set the *keep_settings_over_reset* flag for the drive. When this flag is set, the driver will preserve the -dmu options over a soft reset, as done during the error recovery sequence. This flag defaults to off, to prevent drive reset loops, which could be caused by combinations of -dmu settings. The -k flag should therefore only be set after one has achieved confidence in correct system operation with a chosen set of configuration settings. In practice, all that is typically necessary to test a configuration (prior to using k) is to verify the drive can be read/written, and no error logs (kernel messages) are generated in the process (look in /var/adm/messages on most systems).

- **-K** - Set the drive's *keep_features_over_reset* flag. Setting this enables the drive to retain the settings for -APSWXZ over a soft reset (as done during the error recovery sequence). Not all drives support this feature.

- **-m** - Get/set sector count for multiple sector I/O on the drive. A setting of 0 disables this feature. Multiple sector mode (IDE Block Mode) is a feature of most modern IDE hard drives, permitting the transfer of multiple sectors per I/O interrupt, rather than the usual one sector per interrupt. When this feature is enabled, it typically reduces operating system overhead for disk I/O by 30-50%. On many systems, it also provides increased data throughput of anywhere from 5% to 50%. However some drives, most notably the WD Caviar series, seem to run slower with multiple mode enabled. Your mileage may vary. Most drives support the minimum settings of 2, 4, 8, or 16 (sectors). Larger settings may also be possible, depending on the drive. A setting of 16 or 32 seems optimal on many systems. Western Digital recommends lower settings of 4 to 8 on many of their drives, due to tiny (32kB) drive buffers and non-optimized buffering algorithms. The -i flag can be used to find the maximum setting supported by an installed drive (look for *MaxMultSect* in the output). Some drives claim to support multiple mode, but lose data at some settings. Under rare circumstances, such failures can result in massive file system corruption.

- **-M** - Get/set Automatic Acoustic Management (AAM) setting. Most modern disk drives have the ability to speed down the head movements to reduce their noise output. The possible values are between 0 and 254. The quietest setting is 128 (and therefore slowest) and 254 is the fastest (and loudest). Some drives have only two levels (quiet/fast), while others may have different levels between 128 and 254. THIS FEATURE IS EXPERIMENTAL AND NOT WELL TESTED. USE AT YOUR OWN RISK. The faster the head, the better the performance at a cost of a noisier drive.

- **-p** - Attempt to reprogram the IDE interface chipset for the specified PIO mode, or attempt to auto-tune for the "best" PIO mode supported by the drive. This feature is supported in the kernel for only a few "known" chipsets, and even then, the support is iffy at best. Some IDE chipsets are unable to alter the PIO mode for a single drive, in which case this flag may cause the PIO mode for both drives to be set. Many IDE chipsets support either fewer or more than the standard six (0 to 5) PIO modes, so the exact speed setting that is actually implemented will vary by chipset/driver sophistication. Use with extreme caution! This feature includes zero protection for the unwary, and an unsuccessful outcome may result in severe file system corruption!

- **-P** - Set the maximum sector count for the drive's internal pre-fetch mechanism. Not all drives support this feature.

- **-Q** - Set tagged queue depth (1 or greater), or turn tagged queuing off (0). This only works with the newer 2.5.xx (or later) kernels, and only with the few drives that currently support it.

- **-r** - Get/set read-only flag for device. When set/ write operations are not permitted on the device.

- **-S** - Set the standby (spindown) timeout for the drive. This value is used by the drive to determine how long to wait (with no disk activity) before turning off the spindle motor to save power. Under such circumstances, the drive may take as long as 30 seconds to respond to a subsequent disk access, though most drives are much quicker. The encoding of the timeout value is somewhat peculiar. A value of zero means "off". Values from 1 to 240 specify multiples of 5 seconds for timeouts from 5 seconds to 20 minutes. Values from 241 to 251 specify from 1 to 11 units of 30 minutes for timeouts from 30 minutes to 5.5 hours. A value of 252 signifies a timeout of 21 minutes, 253 sets a vendor-defined timeout and 255 is interpreted as 21 minutes plus 15 seconds.

- **-T** - Perform timings of cache reads for benchmark and comparison purposes. For meaningful results, this operation should be repeated 2-3 times on an otherwise inactive system (no other active processes) with at least a few megabytes of free memory. This displays the speed of reading directly from the Linux buffer cache without disk access. This measurement is essentially an indication of the throughput of the processor, cache, and memory of the system under test. If the -t flag is also specified, then a correction factor based on the outcome of -T will be incorporated into the result reported for the -t operation.

- **-t** - Perform timings of device reads for benchmark and comparison purposes. For meaningful results, this operation should be repeated 2-3 times on an otherwise inactive system (no other active processes) with at least a couple of megabytes of free memory. This displays the speed of reading through the buffer cache to the disk without any prior caching of data. This measurement is an indication of how fast the drive can sustain sequential data reads under Linux, without any file system overhead. To ensure accurate measurements, the buffer cache is flushed during the processing of -t using the BLKFLSBUF *ioctl.* If the -T flag is also specified, then a correction factor based on the outcome of -T will be incorporated into the result reported for the -t operation.

- **-u** - Get/set interrupt-unmask flag for the drive. A setting of 1 permits the driver to unmask other interrupts during processing of a disk interrupt, which greatly improves Linux's responsiveness and eliminates "serial port overrun" errors. Use this feature with caution. Some drive/controller combinations do not tolerate the increased I/O latencies possible when this feature is enabled, resulting in massive file system corruption. In particular, CMD-640B and RZ1000 (E)IDE interfaces can be unreliable (due to a hardware flaw) when this option is used with kernel versions earlier than 2.0.13. Disabling the IDE pre-fetch feature of these interfaces, (usually a BIOS/CMOS setting) provides a safe fix for the problem for use with earlier kernels.

- **-v** - Display all settings, except -i (same as -acdgkmnru for IDE, -gr for SCSI or -adgr for XT). This is also the default behavior when no flags are specified.

- **-W** - Disable/enable the IDE drive's write-caching feature (default state is undeterminable; manufacturer/model specific).

- **-X** - Set the IDE transfer mode for newer (E)IDE/ATA drives. This is typically used in combination with -d1 when enabling DMA to/from a drive on a supported interface chipset. X mdma2 is used to select multiword DMA mode2 transfers and -X sdma1 is used to select simple mode 1 DMA transfers. With systems that support UltraDMA burst timings, -X udma2 is used to select UltraDMA mode2 transfers, (you'll need to prepare the chipset for UltraDMA beforehand). Apart from that, use of this flag is seldom necessary since most/all modern IDE drives default to their fastest PIO transfer mode at power-on. Fiddling with this can be both needless and risky. On drives which support alternate transfer modes, -X can be used to switch the mode of the drive only. Prior to changing the transfer mode, the IDE interface should be jumpered or programmed (see -p flag) for the new mode setting to prevent loss and/or corruption of data. Use this with extreme caution! For the PIO (Programmed Input/Output) transfer modes used by Linux, this value is simply the desired PIO mode number plus 8. Thus, a value of 09 sets PIO mode1, 10 enables PIO mode2, and 11 selects PIO mode3. Setting 00 restores the drive's "default" PIO mode, and 01 disables IORDY. For multiword DMA, the value used is the desired DMA mode number plus 32. For UltraDMA, the value is the desired UltraDMA mode number plus 64.

- **-z** - Force a kernel re-read of the partition table of the specified device(s).

Notes:

As noted above, the -m *sectcount* and -u 1 options should be used with caution at first, preferably on a read-only file system. Most drives work well with these features, but a few drive/controller combinations are not 100% compatible. File system corruption may result. Backup everything before experimenting!

"One more time, folks...don't forget to backup!"

Some options (e.g., -r for SCSI) may not work with old kernels as necessary *ioctl()*'s were not supported.

Although this utility is intended primarily for use with (E)IDE hard disk devices, several of the options are also valid (and permitted) for use with SCSI hard disk devices and MFM/RLL hard disks with XT interfaces.

(The above list of parameters and notes derived from the Linux *man* (manual) pages)

As you can see, we can alter or control about every aspect of the ATA/IDE drive environment and report on some aspects (-r for read-only status and -g for geometry, as well as the -T and -t testing parameters) of the SCSI environment on Linux using the *hdparm* command.

Let's go through an example disk tuning on a LINUX server using *hdparm*.

We have just installed a brand new 40 Gb EIDE disk drive into our Linux server (aultlinux2). Knowing about the *hdparm* command, we run it against the disk after we have configured it for use:

```
[root@aultlinux2 root]# hdparm /dev/hdb

/dev/hdb:
 multcount     = 16 (on)
 IO_support    =  0 (default 16-bit)
 unmaskirq     =  0 (off)
 using_dma     =  0 (off)
 keepsettings  =  0 (off)
 readonly      =  0 (off)
 readahead     =  8 (on)
 geometry      = 77557/16/63, sectors = 78177792, start = 0
```

This doesn't look very good. After all, this is a fairly new drive and should have lots of good features, let's do a -Tt check (give us the performance corrected for any buffering effects):

```
[root@aultlinux2 root]# hdparm -Tt /dev/hdb
/dev/hdb:
 Timing buffer-cache reads:  128 MB in  1.63 seconds = 78.53 MB/sec
 Timing buffered disk reads:  64 MB in 14.20 seconds =  4.51 MB/sec
```

It is, as we feared, 4.51 MB/sec is very poor performance for this drive. It is supposed to give at least 10 MB/sec and usually much more! First, we will leave things as is except we will goose up the IO support from 16 bit to 32 bit (the c1 setting):

```
[root@aultlinux2 root]# hdparm -c1 -u0 -p -d0 /dev/hdb

/dev/hdb:
 attempting to set PIO mode to 0
 setting 32-bit IO_support flag to 1
 setting unmaskirq to 0 (off)
 setting using_dma to 0 (off)
 IO_support   =  1 (32-bit)
 unmaskirq    =  0 (off)
 using_dma    =  0 (off)
[root@aultlinux2 root]# hdparm -Tt /dev/hdb

/dev/hdb:
 Timing buffer-cache reads:  128 MB in  1.63 seconds = 78.53 MB/sec
 Timing buffered disk reads:  64 MB in  9.80 seconds =  6.53 MB/sec
```

Well, a 6.53/4.51*100=144.8 percent improvement with just one setting! Let's make sure it is doing a proper multi-read of 16. We know the controller is capable of DMA2 level support (mdma2), and in order to turn on DMA support, we will need to use the d1 setting and the -X setting to set the proper DMA level. While we are at it, lets set the unmask IRQ setting, so IO is enhanced.

```
[root@aultlinux2 root]# hdparm -m16 -c3 -X mdma2 -d1 -a8 -u1
/dev/hdb

/dev/hdb:
 setting fs readahead to 8
 setting 32-bit IO_support flag to 3
 setting multcount to 16
 setting unmaskirq to 1 (on)
 setting using_dma to 1 (on)
 setting xfermode to 34 (multiword DMA mode2)
 multcount    = 16 (on)
 IO_support   =  3 (32-bit w/sync)
 unmaskirq    =  1 (on)
 using_dma    =  1 (on)
 readahead    =  8 (on)
[root@aultlinux2 root]# hdparm -Tt /dev/hdb
```

```
/dev/hdb:
 Timing buffer-cache reads:  128 MB in  1.56 seconds = 82.05 MB/sec
 Timing buffered disk reads:  64 MB in  4.29 seconds = 14.92 MB/sec
```

All right! That's much better! A 14.92/4.51*100 = 330.8 percent improvement in throughput! On this one's companion drive, /dev/hda, (from a different manufacturer), we were able to get it from 2.15 MB/sec to a whopping 25.7 MB/sec (that's over 1000 percent improvement)!

You will need to add the settings to your startup scripts (usually put it in the database start or Oracle kernel configuration script you use) since they will not be retained between reboots. In addition, you should add the -K flag to retain the settings between soft resets of the drive.

Even if you are only using the ATA drives for system software and swap area, you can see where tuning them using *hdparm* can make a significant performance difference for your system

Tuning the SCSI Interface

SCSI can be used on virtually all systems, NT, Windows 2000, Linux, UNIX, AIX, you name it. SCSI is the most widely used disk interface method going. However, there is virtually no ability to tune the actual interface. There are only a couple of basic parameters that you or your SA can use to affect a change in the performance of the interface itself.

Tuning the SCSI Interface in Windows

There are two ways to change the SCSI settings for a Windows SCSI system. The first is during the install of the driver or during a reboot, usually the system will provide you with a way to get into the SCSI configuration utility when it starts up. The second is via registry edit. Registry edit is a frightening method to do anything in Windows, one wrong entry could result in your system not starting properly or in data corruption or loss. Now that I've scared you, let's discuss the registry edit method for adjusting your SCSI interface.

The items that can be tuned in Windows are located in (or added to) the registry key:

`\HKEY_LOCAL_MACHINE\SYSTEM\CurrentControlSet\Services\aic78xx`

The "aic78xx" is replaced with the name of your controllers driver. The values that can be edited will usually have to be added as values:

DisableTaggedQueuing - A non-zero value disables tagged queuing for SCSI devices. Do not turn off tagged queuing! Tagged queuing improves performance in most situations. This is a REG_SZ data type. (binary)

DisableSynchronousTransfers - A non-zero value indicates that the SCSI host adapter is not to initiate synchronous negotiations, but can accept negotiations from a SCSI target node. This is a REG_SZ data type. (binary)

DisableDisconnects - A nonzero value indicates that targets are not able to disconnect during a transfer. This is data type REG_DWORD. (DWORD)

MaximumLogicalUnit - This can limit the scan for connected devices on the SCSI bus. Values are 1-8. If 1 is specified then the SCSI manager assumes no LUNs greater than 0 are present. This is data type REG_DWORD. (DWORD)

MaximumSGList - Specifies the maximum number of Scatter/Gather elements. The valid range of values is 17-255. This one's data type is REG_DWORD. (DWORD)

These values are added by using the following procedure:

1. Click on the *Start* button.

2. Select the *Run* menu item

3. In the *Run* dialog box, enter the appropriate registry editor name (may be *regedit32* or just *regedit*)

4. Press the *Enter* key

5. Open the registry list to the appropriate location, for example:

```
\HKEY_LOCAL_MACHINE\SYSTEM\CurrentControlSet\Services\<driver>\
Parameters\Device
```

6. If the keys (Parameters and Device) listed above do not exist, you will have to add them by right clicking on the driver name and selecting the proper drop-down boxes. See Figure 3.5.

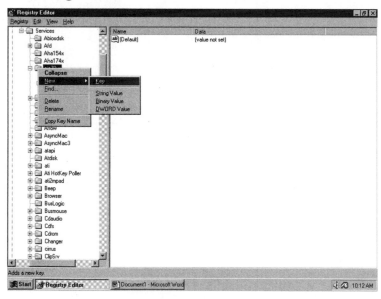

Figure 3.5: *Adding a Key*

7. To add a specific host adapter append *Device* with its indicator, device zero would be *Device0*. If the number is not specified the configuration information applies to all SCSI family host devices.

8. Right click on the *Device* key.

9. Select *Add Value* from the *Edit* menu. In the *Value Name* edit box, enter one of the valid parameter values. Make sure to enter the appropriate data type for the value and make sure you use the proper case exactly as they are specified. Repeat 8 and 9 for all additional keys. See Figure 3.6.

Figure 3.6: *Adding Values to the Device Key*

There are additional device specific parameters that can also be modified or added. These are:

- **/INSTRUMENTATION** - enables recording of I/O statistics and errors. If this option is not specified, instrumentation defaults to disabled. Instrumentation is nice for trouble shooting, but does cost CPU and IO cycles, so only turn it on when needed. This is data type REG_SZ

- **/INSTR_ERRLOG_Z=nnn** - This sets the maximum number of error log entries to maintain, and defaults to 32. The valid range is 1-128. This is data type REG_SZ.

- **/MAXTAGS=nnn** - This specifies the tagged queue depth. If a number is not specified the tagged queue depth defaults to 128. The valid range is 1-255. The larger the value in most cases, the more commands can be aggregated and performance is improved. The data type for this is REG_SZ. This is probably the most important parameter for performance.

- **/HOTPLUG** - This enables the capability to use hot-plug PCI features. This will default to no hot-plug capability if not specified. This item has no value; it is just a tag.

These are added to a new parameter added at the device level called DeviceParameters, which is a string value. The parameters are added as a space separated list. See Figure 3.7.

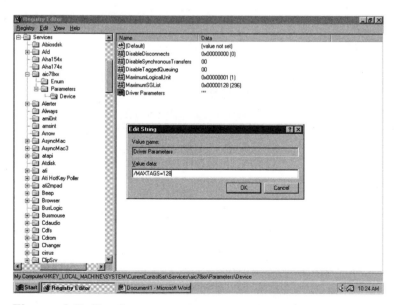

Figure 3.7: Device *DriverParameters Value*

You need to look at your adapter manual (you may have to download a copy from the device manufacturer's website) for the parameters that can be added or modified for your adapter.

SCSI Tuning Under Linux

Under Linux, the SCSI interface is tuned either by specifying parameters in the boot command of the Grub or Lilo boot file or by specifying options in the /etc/modules.conf file. Let's look at examples of both of these. The relative performance of the interface can be measured in Linux using the *hdparm* command with the -Tt option. Note that the IEEE1394 interface is treated as a SCSI interface in Linux. The following examples are for tuning the generic SBP2 interface, but the techniques can also be supplied to specific SCSI drivers.

First, let's look at the current settings for the interface. You get those by looking under the LUN number in the /proc/scsi/sbp2 directory. This example used LUN 0.

```
[root@aultlinux1 root]# cat /proc/scsi/sbp2/0
IEEE-1394 SBP-2 protocol driver (host: ohci1394)
$Rev: 601 $ James Goodwin <jamesg@filanet.com>
SBP-2 module load options:
- Max speed supported: S400
- Max sectors per I/O supported: 255
- Max outstanding commands supported: 0
- Max outstanding commands per lun supported: 1
- Serialized I/O (debug): no
- Exclusive login: no
```

Now we run a timing test to determine the average speed for the interface as-is (run this several times and average the results):

```
/dev/sda:
 Timing buffer-cache reads:  128 MB in  3.99 seconds = 32.08 MB/sec
 Timing buffered disk reads:  64 MB in  6.86 seconds =  9.33 MB/sec
[root@aultlinux1 root]# hdparm -Tt /dev/sda
```

Now we will set the values for the SBP2 options in the /etc/modules.conf file. We are doubling the outstanding commands to 16 and increasing the commands per LUN to 2:

```
alias parport_lowlevel parport_pc
alias eth0 3c59x
alias usb-controller usb-ohci
alias eth1 tulip
alias ieee1394-controller ohci1394
alias scsi_hostadapter sbp2
options sbp2 sbp2_max_outstanding_cmds=16 sbp2_max_cmds_per_lun=2
```

Now we reboot so the settings will take effect, then re-check our settings in /proc/scsi/sbp2/0:

```
[root@aultlinux1 root]# cat /proc/scsi/sbp2/0
IEEE-1394 SBP-2 protocol driver (host: ohci1394)
$Rev: 601 $ James Goodwin <jamesg@filanet.com>
SBP-2 module load options:
- Max speed supported: S400
- Max sectors per I/O supported: 255
- Max outstanding commands supported: 16
- Max outstanding commands per lun supported: 2
- Serialized I/O (debug): no
- Exclusive login: no
```

Our settings have been modified, now let's re-run the timing test:

```
[root@aultlinux1 etc]# hdparm -Tt /dev/sda

/dev/sda:
 Timing buffer-cache reads:  128 MB in  4.03 seconds = 35.36 MB/sec
 Timing buffered disk reads:  64 MB in  6.04 seconds = 11.25 MB/sec
```

From a simple modification, we improved SCSI speed for this device by 11.25/9.33*100= 120.6 percent. Overall, a 20% speed improvement. Subsequently we doubled, quadrupled and eventually got to a setting of 255 for the maximum outstanding commands, the performance peaked at 11.25 MB/sec with 16 as a setting. If the servers being tuned are in a cluster, all of them should have the same settings.

Tuning SCSI Under UNIX

SCSI tuning under UNIX is dependent on the version of UNIX involved and the SCSI card or motherboard interface being tuned. Let's look at SUN.

On any system, SUN included, the system bus has a fixed bandwidth. If there are too many devices on the bus this will result in more traffic than the bus can handle, which then results in contention and packet loss.

In the SUN Solaris operating system, the *prtdiag -v* command is used to report on the system bus configuration. By adding up the reported capacities of the devices on the bus reported by *prtdiag —v,* and seeing if they exceed the capacity of the bus, it is possible to see if the bus is overloaded.

Whenever possible, similar cards should be placed on the same board so the interrupts are directed to the same CPU (and associated caches).

Table 3.1 shows some typical SUN system bus capacities:

BUS	SPEED	WIDTH	BURST BANDWIDTH	SUSTAINED BANDWIDTH
MBus	33MHz	64 bit	264 MB/s	86 MB/s
MBus	36MHz	64 bit	288 MB/s	94 MB/s
MBus	40MHz	64 bit	320 MB/s	105 MB/s
MBus	50MHz	64 bit	400 MB/s	130 MB/s
XDBus	40MHz	64 bit	320 MB/s	250 MB/s
XDBus	50MHz	64 bit	400 MB/s	312 MB/s
UPA	72MHz	128 bit	1.15 GB/s	1 GB/s
UPA	83.5MHz	128 bit	1.3 GB/s	1.2 GB/s
UPA	100MHz	128 bit	1.5 GB/s	1.44 GB/s

Gigaplane	83.5MHz	256 bit	2.6 GB/s	2.5 GB/s
GigaplaneXB	100MHz	1024 bit	12.8 GB/s	12.8 GB/s

Table 3.1: *Typical Bus Capacities*

Peripheral Buses

The two peripheral buses on Sun systems are Sbus and PCI bus. Sbus typically runs at 20-25MHz and provides 32 or 64 bit sizes. The peak Sbus bandwidth is 200 MB/s. The PCI bus runs at 33 or 66MHz and may be 32 or 64 bit. The peak PCI bus bandwidth is 528 MB/s. Almost all add-on SCSI adapters will plug into the PCI bus.

SCSI Bus

SCSI buses on SUN can operate various bandwidths, speeds and throughputs (see Table 3.2 to see the various bus specifications for SUN). The *prtconf* Solaris command is used to report information that can be used to determine the speed of a particular SCSI device. Most of the SCSI systems I have seen in recent years have been SCSI3 based.

PROTOCOL	BUS WIDTH	BUS SPEED	THROUGHPUT
SCSI1	8bit	5MHz	5MB/s
Fast SCSI, SCSI2	8bit	10MHz	10MB/s
Fast Wide SCSI, SCSI3	16bit	10MHz	20MB/s
Ultra SCSI	8bit	20MHz	20MB/s
Wide Ultra SCSI, Fast20	16bit	20MHz	40MB/s
Ultra2 SCSI	8bit	40MHz	40MB/s
Wide Ultra2 SCSI, Fast40	16bit	40MHz	80MB/s

Ultra3, Ultra160, Fast80	16Bit	80MHz	160MB/s
Ultra320, Fast160	16Bit	80MHz	320MB/s

Table 3.2: *SUN SCSI Specifications*

The *scsi_options* parameter can be set in the /etc/system file to limit bus speed or set other characteristics. You should check device documentation to determine if these settings need to be specified for a specific device. The default *scsi_options* variable allows the widest range of capabilities that the SCSI host adapter can provide to be supported.

The default *scsi_options* value on Solaris 2.x works for both 5MB and 10MB devices. The driver will negotiate with each device to determine if it is 10MB transfer capable or not. If they are 10MB devices, 10MB transfer will be used. If not, 5MB transfer will be used.

SCSI subsystem options - on SUN Solaris, a global word of options are available. The bits of the global word are broken down as:

BIT(S)	USE
0-2	Reserved for debugging/informational level
3	Reserved for a global disconnect/reconnect switch
4	Reserved for a global linked command capability switch
5	Reserved for a global synchronous SCSI capability switch

The rest of the bits are reserved for future use.

The bits which can be set, are set using the hexadecimal values are shown in Table 3.3.

OPTION TAG	OPTION VALUE	DESCRIPTION
SCSI_DEBUG_TGT	0x1	Debug statements in target drivers
SCSI_DEBUG_LIB	0x2	Debug statements in library
SCSI_DEBUG_HA	0x4	Debug statements in host adapters
SCSI_OPTIONS_DR	0x8	Global disconnect/reconnect
SCSI_OPTIONS_LINK	0x10	Global linked commands
SCSI_OPTIONS_SYNC	0x20	Global synchronous xfer capability
SCSI_OPTIONS_PARITY	0x40	Global parity support
SCSI_OPTIONS_TAG	0x80	Tagged command support
SCSI_OPTIONS_FAST	0x100	FAST scsi support
SCSI_OPTIONS_WIDE	0x200	WIDE scsi support

Table 3.3: *SCIS Options Hexadecimal Values*

The values for the various options are added to achieve the desired combination of features,. For example, a line in /etc/system that read:

```
set scsi_options=0x3f8
```

means that the default options would be to allow WIDE SCSI, FAST SCSI, tagged commands, global parity, synchronous transfer, linked commands and global disconnect/reconnect, i.e. all currently supported options.

SCSI chains may be made of single-ended or differential connections. They should not be mixed, as this may damage the equipment. Differential connections permit longer chains, but the hardware is usually more expensive. Single-ended chains must be less than 6 m in length; differential chains must be less than 20 m for synchronous connections or 25 m for asynchronous connections.

A Single ended SCSI connection uses "Normal" electrical signals, and uses an open collector to the SCSI bus. The maximum length for SCSI-1 is a 6 meter cable with stubs of max 10cm, allowed to connect a device to the main-cable. Most devices are single ended.

A differential SCSI connection uses two wires to drive one signal. It has a maximum cable length of 25 meters. Differential SCSI is electrically incompatible with single ended devices, allowed in SCSI-1 and upwards based systems.

The SCSI target numbers represent attachment points on the SCSI chain. Each target number may include as many as 8 devices (luns or logical unit numbers). Embedded SCSI devices only include one lun.

Higher target numbers receive better service and on a narrow bus, the target priorities run 7 -> 0. On a wide bus, they run 7 -> 0, then 15 -> 8. The host adapter is usually 7. This can cause problems where busy disks and tape devices share a SCSI bus, since tape devices are usually assigned target 6. If possible, isolate tape devices to their own SCSI bus.

If you are running older drives with Solaris 2.7 and above, you may run into a situation where there are many bus over-runs and errors. This is usually caused by having one or more disks on the SCSI bus that improperly implement the tagged queuing option (or don't support it at all!).

For a quick fix, append this line to /etc/system and reboot:

```
set scsi_options & ~0x80
```

This turns off the Tagged Command Queuing. Tagged command queuing has also been seen to cause problems between Suns and some RAID implementations. However, the best fix is to replace the older drives with newer drives that will probably offer higher speed and greater capacity anyway.

Nevertheless, verify that your drives are incapable of supporting tagged queuing before making this change, since this will seriously degrade performance on disks that do properly support tagged command queuing. Setting the SCSI options for the target drives that can't support the option is therefore the preferred solution.

In Solaris 2.4 and later versions, you can set those options per SCSI bus. See your systems man entries or paper manual instructions for isp(7) and esp(7).

For some disks, decreasing the maximum number of queued commands by setting an option for the sd driver (SCSI Driver) using the host configuration variable *sd_max_throttle*, is all that is necessary:

```
set sd:sd_max_throttle=10
```

In later Solaris releases, you can specify *scsi_options* per target or per SCSI bus. See esp(7d), isp(7d), from which this example /kernel/drv/esp.conf file is derived:

```
name="esp"
parent="/iommu@f,e0000000/sbus@f,e0001000/espdma@f,400000"
reg=0xf,0x800000,0x40
target1-scsi-options=0x58
scsi-options=0x178;
```

It has also been reported that some hardware RAIDs support a number of different LUNs (logical disks), but these LUNs share a common set of I/O buffers between them. This can cause SCSI QFULL conditions on those devices that do not have commands queued. Since the usual algorithm is to retry the command when a previous command is completed, Solaris doesn't handle this situation very well.

The workaround is to decrease *sd_max_throttle* such that there's always at least 1 slot available for each LUN, e.g., if you have 3 LUNs and your RAID supports a maximum of 64 outstanding commands, *sd_max_throttle* must be at most 31. Any two LUNs can get 31 requests and you still have two slots left over for number 3.

For some hardware RAIDs, it has been found that decreasing *sd_max_throttle* improved performance due to better load balancing among LUNs. It might be worth a shot if your hardware based RAID system seems sluggish.

There are several additional host configuration variables that can be specified in addition to *sd_max_throttle* and in relation to the SCSI interface on SUN Solaris. These are usually specified in the /etc/system file as was shown above.

The following variables in the /etc/systems file should be set to maximize system performance. When any of these variables are changed, the system must be rebooted for changes to take effect.

- *sd_max_throttle* -- The *sd_max_throttle* variable sets the maximum number of commands that the SCSI sd driver will attempt to queue to a single HBA driver. The default value is 256. This variable must be set to a value less than or equal to the maximum queue depth of each LUN connected to each instance of the sd driver. If this is not done, then commands may be rejected because of a full queue condition and the sd driver instance that receives the queue full message will throttle down *sd_max_throttle* to 1. This obviously will result in degraded performance. The variable is set in the /etc/system file as follows:

```
set sd:sd_max_throttle=20
```

- *sd_io_time* -- The *sd_io_time* variable is command time out value. Setting this time out value to 120 seconds will prevent the host from issuing warning messages while non-disruptive operations are performed on the disk array. For example, in a EMC Symmettrix power path environment this variable can be set to 0x3C (60 seconds). As with the *sd_max_throttle* value, this is set in the /etc/system file. Using the EMC value in an example:

```
set sd:sd_io_time = 0x3C
```

- *scsi_options* -- The value *scsi_options* is a setting for SCSI options included as outlined in the bit meaning table above. Solaris 7 default SCSI settings are for the maximum Ultra Wide Speed. Since the /etc/system file can also affect other disks in the system, consider the effects of implementing the *scsi_options*=0x7F8 mask on the other disks. You might consider the bus level or device level setpoints as we discussed above rather than a system wide setting. An example entry in the /etc/system file would be:

```
set scsi_options=0x7F8
```

In addition to the /etc/system file, the file /kernel/drv/sd.conf can also be used to specify SCSI driver specific settings. However, these usually deal with specifying addresses for hardware RAID. For example, you must modify the host configuration file /kernel/drv/sd.conf to insure smooth integration from the host and hardware based RAID or disk systems such as EMC's Symmetrix.

Using Symmetrix as an example, Symmetrix devices are addressed on the Fibre Channel bus using the Symmetrix Hard Loop ID as a Target ID. There is only one Target ID per Symmetrix port. A Target ID can have up to 128 luns. By default, Solaris searches only for Target IDs; if LUN addressing is required, you must modify the file /kernel/drv/sd.conf. However, this isn't a SCSI configuration book, so we aren't going to cover that aspect.

SUN Conclusions for SCSI Interface Tuning

In order to have a properly tuned interface, you must make sure the proper SCSI options are set at the system (/etc/system) and bus as well as device level (*scsi_options*). Make sure that the proper command queued depth (*sd_max_throttle*) and proper command delay times (*sd_io_time*) are set. In a mixed environment (multiple SCSI devices with different queue depths and IO considerations) set these at the device level or the entire SCSI system or bus will be drug down to the performance of the least powerful device. Finally, try to isolate tape or other low speed devices on their own SCSI bus as their device numbers are usually set to 6, which causes them to usurp service from other devices in the chain.

HP-UX SCSI Tuning

Much like SUN Solaris, HP has several kernel based tuning parameters that are used to adjust the behavior of to SCSI interface, bus and device.

Probably, the most important is *scsi_max_qdepth*. *scsi_max_qdepth* is the maximum number of I/Os that a single SCSI target will queue up for execution. The parameters has a minimum value of 1, a default set value of 8, and a maximum value of 255.

Some SCSI devices support tagged queuing, which means they can have more than one SCSI command outstanding at any point in time. The number of commands that can be outstanding varies by device and is not known to HP-UX. To avoid overflowing this queue, HP-UX will not send more than a certain number of outstanding commands to any SCSI device. This tunable sets the default value for that limit. The default value can be overridden for specific devices using *ioctl*. The *ioctl* is a device interface system control that allows commands to be issued to alter specific setpoints on devices; it is not a command line program.

Queue depth is synonymous to the tagged command queuing in other systems. When tagged command queuing is supported by a target, it allows the target to accept multiple SCSI commands for execution. By accepting multiple commands, intelligent on-disk controllers can optimize how the commands are carried out by positioning reads and writes in the order to minimize disk head movement between operations. Some targets can allow up to 256 commands to be stored from different initiators. Once the target command queue is full, the target terminates any additional I/O and returns a QUEUE FULL status to the initiator. Some older targets may support less than 256 commands to be queued, and this is the reason the setting defaults to 8. Why the value is set so low is not explained.

If the system has a combination of devices that support small and larger queue depths, then a queue depth can be set to a value, which would work for most devices. For specific devices, the system administrator can change the queue depth on a per device basis using *sio_set_lun_limit* in *ioctl()*. See the

HP-UX manual entries on *scsictl*(1M) for more on how to use *ioctl()*.

This value should only be raised in SCSI devices that have enough memory to support higher queue depth than the default set by HP. Such devices may offer better performance if the queue depth is set to a higher value.

Remember, the queue depth applies to all the SCSI devices that support tag queuing. Setting the queue depth to a value larger than the disk can handle will result in I/Os being held off once a QUEUE FULL condition exists on the disk. A mechanism exists that will lower the queue depth of the device in case of QUEUE FULL condition avoiding infinite QUEUE FULL conditions on that device similar to the process that lowers it to 1 on SUN Solaris. Nevertheless, this mechanism will periodically try higher queue depths and QUEUE FULL conditions will arise.

This parameter should be lowered when the connected SCSI devices support smaller queue depth or for load balancing. However, devices that support higher queue depth may not deliver optimal performance when a lower queue depth value is set.

The other tunable parameter in HP-UX for SCSI is *scsi_maxphys*, which sets the maximum allowed length of an IO on all SCSI devices. *scsi_maxphys* has a minimum and maximum setting of 1048576 (one megabyte) except on V-class systems, where it has the range of values: 16777215 and 33554432.

This tunable parameter sets the maximum data size the SCSI subsystem will accept for an I/O. Depending on the device's characteristics and the device driver configuration, the maximum size allowed by the SCSI subsystem for a particular SCSI device might be lower than or equal to this tunable parameters value. It will never be greater.

The only time this parameter can be adjusted above one megabyte is when you have a V-Class system where it can be raised to 32 MB.

The *scsictl* command allows adjustment of the parameters for SCSI on a HP-UX platform. The basic format for the *scsictl* command is:

```
scsictl [-akq] [-c command]... [-m mode[= value]]... device
```

The *scsictl* command recognizes the options listed in Table 3.4.

OPTION	SUB-OPTIONS & DESCRIPTIONS	
-a	Display the status of all mode parameters available, separated by semicolon-blank (;) or newline.	
-c command	Cause the device to perform the specified command. Command can be one of the following:	
	erase	For magneto-optical devices that support write without erase, this command can be used to pre-erase the whole surface to increase data throughput on subsequent write operations. This command maintains exclusive access to the surface during the pre-erasure.
	sync_cache	For devices that have an internal write cache, this command causes the device to flush its cache to the physical medium.

OPTION	SUB-OPTIONS & DESCRIPTIONS
domain_val	Domain validation allows the user to check the quality of transmissions across the bus and helps to find problems like faulty and missing terminators, bad components, etc. This command is only valid for Ultra160 and later devices. If any errors encountered during domain validation, they will be logged in the syslog.
get_bus_parms	This command displays information about limits and negotiable parameters of a bus.
get_lun_parms	This command displays information about limits and negotiable parameters of a physical or a virtual peripheral device.
get_target_parms	This command displays information about limits and negotiable parameters of a target peripheral device.
reset_target	This command causes a target reset task management function to be sent to the associated target.

OPTION	SUB-OPTIONS & DESCRIPTIONS	
	reset_bus	This command causes the system to generate a SCSI bus reset condition on the associated bus. A SCSI bus reset condition causes all devices on the bus to be reset (including clearing all active commands on all devices).
-k	Continue processing arguments even after an error is detected. The default behavior is to exit immediately when an error is detected. Command line syntax is always verified for correctness, regardless of the -k option. Improper command line syntax causes scsictl to exit without performing any operations on the device.	
-m mode	Display the status of the specified mode parameter. Mode can be one of the following:	
	immediate_report	For devices that support immediate reporting, this mode controls how the device responds to write requests. If immediate report is enabled (1), write requests can be acknowledged before the data is physically transferred to the media. If immediate report is disabled (0), the device is forced to await the completion of any write request before reporting its status.
	Ir	Equivalent to immediate_report.

OPTION	SUB-OPTIONS & DESCRIPTIONS
queue_depth	For devices that support a queue depth greater than the system default, this mode controls how many I/Os the driver will attempt to queue to the device at any one time. Valid values are (1-255). Some disk devices will not support the maximum queue depth settable by this command. Setting the queue depth in software to a value larger than the disk can handle will result in I/Os being held off once a QUEUE FULL condition exists on the disk.
	Set the mode parameter mode to value. The available mode parameters and values are listed above. Mode parameters that take only a binary value (1 or 0) and can also be specified as either on or off, respectively.
-q	Suppress the labels that are normally printed when mode parameters are displayed. Mode parameter values are printed in the same order as they appear on the command line, separated by semicolon-blank (;) or newline.

Figure 3.4: *The scsictl Command Options*

Mode parameters and commands need only be specified up to a unique prefix. When abbreviating a mode parameter or command, at least the first three characters must be supplied.

To display all the mode parameters, turn *immediate_report* on, and redisplay the value of *immediate_report*:

```
scsictl -a -m ir=1 -m ir /dev/rdsk/c0t6d0
```

This produces the following output:

```
immediate_report = 0; queue_depth = 8;
immediate_report = 1
```

To get the same output using the suppression of labels, the command would look like so:

```
scsictl -aq -m ir=1 -m ir /dev/rdsk/c0t6d0
```

This produces the following output:

```
0; 8; 1
```

Remember, when the system is rebooted, the HP-UX *disk3* and *sdisk* drivers always reset the value of the *immediate_report* mode parameter to OFF. If *ioctl* or *scsictl* is used to change the setting of immediate reporting on a SCSI device, the new value becomes the default setting upon subsequent configuration (e.g., opens) of this device and retains its value across system or device powerfail recovery. However, on the next system reboot, the *immediate_report* mode parameter is reset to the value of the tunable system parameter, *default_disk_ir*. This parameter is set in the *system_file* used to create the HP-UX system by the *config* command.

SCSI Tuning Under AIX

AIX is a SCO UNIX derivative like HP-UX (Solaris is a SVR4 UNIX derivative). However, AIX has been highly modified from the standard SCO release of UNIX, unlike HP-UX, which remains fairly true to the original SCO. The SCSI interface in AIX has several parameters that can be adjusted. Generally speaking, the IBM disks can be read by the interface and adjustments are usually made automatically, after market drives (that is, non-IBM manufacture), may need to have proper settings made manually. Let's look at the available settings in AIX.

Setting AIX SCSI-Adapter and Disk-Device Queue Limits

The AIX operating system, like LINUX, Windows and HP-UX, has the ability to enforce limits on the number of I/O requests that can be outstanding from the SCSI adapter to a given SCSI bus or disk drive. These limits are intended to exploit the hardware's ability to handle multiple requests while ensuring that the seek-optimization algorithms in the device drivers are able to operate effectively.

For non-IBM devices, it is sometimes required to modify AIX default queue-limit values to ensure highest performance rather than use those that have been chosen to handle the worst possible case. Let's look at situations in which the defaults should be changed and the IBM recommended new values.

AIX SCSI Settings With a Non-IBM Disk Drive

The default settings for AIX for IBM disk drives for the number of requests that can be outstanding at any given time is 3 (8 for SSA). This value has no direct interface for changing it. The default hardware queue depth for non-IBM disk drives is a very performance killing 1. It behooves you to change the setting for Non-IBM drives if they can accept multiple commands (most modern drives can), so you can get the maximum performance from those drives. For example, you can display the default characteristics of a non-IBM disk drive with the *lsattr* command:

```
# lsattr -D -c disk -s scsi -t osdisk

pvid          none Physical volume identifier      False
clr_q         no    Device CLEARS its Queue on error
q_err         yes   Use QERR bit
q_type        simple Queuing TYPE
queue_depth   3     Queue DEPTH
reassign_to   120   REASSIGN time out value
rw_timeout    30    READ/WRITE time out value
start_timeout 60    START unit time out value
```

You should use the AIX provided interface, *SMIT* to change the disk parameters as required. *SMIT* allows for fast-pathing to specific points in the SMIT interface from the command line. The fast path is *smitty chgdsk* to get the disk interface section of *SMIT*. As an alternative, you can also use the *chdev* command line command to change these parameters.

Let's look at an example using *chdev*, if your system contained a non-IBM SCSI disk drive hdisk7, the following command enables queuing for that device and sets its queue depth to 3:

```
# chdev -l hdisk7 -a q_type=simple -a queue_depth=3
```

That's fine for a single disk, but what about when you are dealing with an entire non-IBM disk array? Let's look at that next.

Setting SCSI Parameters for a Non-IBM Disk Array

Any disk array appears to AIX as a single, rather large, disk drive. A non-IBM disk array, like a non-IBM disk drive, will be of class *disk*, subclass *scsi*, type *osdisk* (which is short for "Other SCSI Disk Drive"). However, we know a disk array actually contains a number of physical disk drives. Each physical disk drive can handle multiple requests, therefore the

---

queue depth for the disk array device has to be set to a value high enough to allow efficient use of all of the physical devices. For example, if hdisk8 were an eight-disk non-IBM disk array, where each disk supports a queued depth of 3, an appropriate change using *chdev* would be:

```
# chdev -l hdisk8 -a q_type=simple -a queue_depth=24
```

If the disk array is attached via a SCSI-2 Fast/Wide SCSI adapter bus, it may also be necessary to change the outstanding-request limit for that bus. Let's look at that next.

Changing AIX Disk Adapter Outstanding-Request Limits

The AIX SCSI-2 Fast/Wide Adapter supports two SCSI buses, one for internal devices and one for external devices. There is a limit on the total number of outstanding requests that can be defined for each bus. The default value of that limit is 40 for each bus and the maximum is 128. When an IBM disk array is attached to a SCSI-2 Fast/Wide Adapter bus, the outstanding-request limit for the bus is increased automatically to accommodate the queue depth of the disk array. However, for a non-IBM disk array, this change must be performed manually. For example, using *chdev* to set the outstanding-request limit of adapter *scsi2* to 80, you would use:

```
# chdev -l scsi2 -a num_cmd_elems=80
```

Note, if you are using the SCSI-2 High Performance Controller, the maximum number of queued requests is 30 and that limit cannot be changed. For that reason, you should ensure the sum of the queue depths of the devices attached to a SCSI-2 High Performance Controller does not exceed 30.

You should also note that the original RS/6000 SCSI adapter does not support queuing. It is inappropriate to attach a disk array device to such an adapter.

Controlling the Number of System pbufs in AIX

In AIX the Logical Volume Manager (LVM) uses a construct called a "pbuf" to control a pending I/O to disk. In AIX Version 3, one pbuf is required for each page being read or written. In systems that do large amounts of sequential I/O, this can result in depletion of the pool of pbufs. The *vmtune* command can be used to increase the number of pbufs to compensate for this effect.

In AIX Version 4, only a single pbuf is used for each sequential I/O request, *regardless* of the number of pages involved. This greatly decreases the probability of running out of pbufs and tuning pbufs in version 4 and is generally not advised.

In AIX Version 5, you no longer need to adjust this parameter.

Tuning the IEEE1394 Interface

Usually the IEEE1394 interface is only used in Windows, Apple or LINUX environments. In these environments it is treated as a subset of the SCSI interface and is tuned accordingly. In fact, the example used for tuning the SCSI interface in LINUX, shown previously in this chapter, is actually a session used to tune the IEEE1394 interface.

Tuning the Fibre Channel Interface

As the Fibre Channel interface is actually a "highway" for other interfaces to use, it generally requires no tuning. To use it efficiently, you tune it by tuning the other interfaces.

Conclusion

Tuning disk interfaces generally involves controlling the number of commands that are sent to each disk on the interface. These commands are controlled via the mechanism of queued command depths where the number of commands sent to either a bus or device is preset to prevent command overflows. Another setting throttles the total flow of commands on the bus to individual devices and provides for load balancing (*sd_max_throttle* for example). When the disk interface senses errors, it usually throttles back to the minimal settings (usually 1), which can severely inhibit performance.

References

IEEE1394 Firewire/ilink, XILINX, ESP - Emerging Standards and Protocols, PowerPoint Presentation, www.xilinx.com

www.westerndigital.com FAQ section

www.seagate.com

www.princeton.edu/~unix/Solaris/troubleshoot/diskio.html

SunSolve Document, ID: 1227

QLogic Corporation QLA2100F PCI Fibre Channel Adapter, RELEASE NOTES FOR SYMMETRIX ICDA SYSTEM UPDATED: July 27, 1999

HP-UX Reference, HP-UX 11i Version 1.6, Customer Order Number: ONLINE ONLY, HP Part Number:B3921-90010, June 2002, Printed in USA, Copyright 1983-2002 Hewlett-Packard Company. All rights reserved.

AIX Versions 3.2 and 4 Performance Tuning Guide, Fifth Edition (April 1996), IBM Corp.

AIX 5L Version 5.1, Performance Management Guide, Third Edition (April 2002), Copyright International Business Machines Corporation 1997, 2002

RAID Technology

Disk Striping

Unless you've been living in seclusion from the computer mainstream, you will have heard of disk striping, shadowing, and RAID. Let's take a brief look at them and how they are used in Oracle.

Disk striping is the process by which multiple smaller disks are made to look like one large disk. This allows extremely large databases, or even extremely large single-table tablespaces, to occupy one logical device. This makes managing the resource easier since backups only have to address one logical volume instead of several. This also provides the advantage of spreading I/O across several disks. If you will need several ten's or hundred's of gigabytes of disk storage for your application, striping is the way to go. One disadvantage to striping: If one of the disks in the set crashes, you lose them all unless you have a high-reliability array with hot swap capability. Striping is RAID 0.

Figure 4.1 shows an example of 4 disks using 3 stripes per disk. This allows larger logical disks that would be allowed from a single disk. It also spreads the data across more platters allowing a higher IO rate. All of the stripe 1 slices form one logical disk, as do all of the stripe 3 slices and the stripe 3 slices, so we have created 3 larger logical disks with 4 times the possible IO rate of any of the disks individually.

Disk Striping

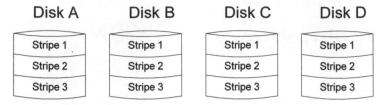

Figure 4.1: *Example of Disk Striping*

Disk Shadowing or Mirroring

If you have mission-critical applications that you absolutely cannot allow to go down, consider disk shadowing or mirroring. As its name implies, disk shadowing or mirroring is the process whereby each disk has a shadow or mirror disk that data is written to simultaneously. This redundant storage allows the shadow disk or set of disks to pick up the load in case of a disk crash on the primary disk or disks; thus the users never see a crashed disk. Once the disk is brought back on-line, the shadow or mirror process brings it back in sync by a process appropriately called "resilvering." This also allows for backup since the shadow or mirror set can be broken (e.g., the shadow separated from the primary), a backup taken, and then the set resynchronized. There have been two, three, and even higher mirror sets. Generally, there is no reason for more than a three-way mirror as this allows for the set of three to be broken into a single and a double set for backup purposes. Shadowing or Mirroring is RAID 1.

Did someone say something about mirroring?

The main disadvantage to disk shadowing is the cost: For a 200-GB disk farm, you need to purchase 400 or more gigabytes of disk storage. Figure 4.2 shows disk mirroring. Disk group A is considered the active group, disk group B is the "mirror" group. Both disk group A and disk group B are maintained through simultaneous writes.

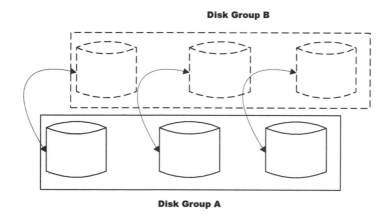

Figure 4.2: *Example of Disk Mirroring*

So far we have discussed basic RAID technology (RAID - Redundant Arrays of Inexpensive Disks.) RAID can be either software based or hardware based. Software based RAID never performs as well as hardware based RAID, in some cases software RAID actually performs worse than individual disks. RAID controllers are readily available so there is no need to depend on software RAID.

RAID—Redundant Arrays of Inexpensive Disks

The main strengths of RAID technology are its dependability and IO bandwidth. For example, in a RAID5 array, the data is stored, as are checksums and other information about the contents of each disk in the array. If one disk is lost, the others can use this stored information to re-create the lost data. However, this rebuild of data on-the-fly causes a massive hit on performance. In RAID 1, RAID 10 and RAID 01 failed disks are immediately replaced by their mirror with no performance hit. This makes RAID very attractive. RAID 5 has the same advantages as shadowing and striping at a lower cost. It has been suggested that if the manufacturers would use slightly more expensive disks (RASMED—redundant array of slightly more expensive disks) performance gains could be realized. A RAID system appears as one very large, reliable disk to the CPU. There are several levels of RAID to date:

- **RAID 0**. Known as disk striping.

- **RAID 1**. Known as disk shadowing or mirroring.

- **RAID 0/1**. Combination of RAID0 and RAID1. May also be called RAID 10 depending on whether they are striped and mirrored or mirrored then striped. It is generally felt that RAID 10 performs better than RAID 01.

- **RAID 2**. Data is distributed in extremely small increments across all disks and adds one or more disks that contain a Hamming code for redundancy. RAID 2 is not considered commercially viable due to the added disk requirements (10 to 20 percent must be added to allow for the Hamming disks).

- **RAID 3**. This also distributes data in small increments but adds only one parity disk. This results in good performance for large transfers, but small transfers show poor performance.

- **RAID 4**. In order to overcome the small transfer performance penalties in RAID3, RAID4 uses large data chunks distributed over several disks and a single parity disk. This results in a bottleneck at the parity disk. Due to this performance problem RAID 4 is not considered commercially viable. RAID 3 and 4 are usually are used for video streaming technology or large LOB storage.

- **RAID 5**. This solves the bottleneck by distributing the parity data across the disk array. The major problem is it requires several write operations to update parity data. The performance hit is only moderate, and the other benefits may outweigh this minor problem. However, the penalty for writes can be over 20% and must be weighed against the benefits.

- **RAID 6**. This adds a second redundancy disk that contains error-correction codes. Read performance is good due to load balancing, but write performance suffers due to RAID 6 requiring more writes than RAID 5 for data update.

For the money, RAID0/1 or RAID1/0, that is, striped and mirrored is suggested. It provides nearly all of the dependability of RAID5 and gives much better write performance. You will usually take at least a 20 percent write performance hit using RAID5. For read-only applications

RAID5 is a good choice, but in high-transaction/high-performance environments the write penalties may be too high. Figure 4.3 shows RAID 1-0 or 0-1 depending on whether you stripe and then mirror or mirror first and then stripe. In most situations you get better performance from RAID 1-0 (mirroring then striping.)

Disk Group 2

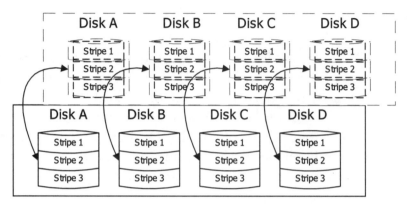

Disk Group 1

Figure 4.3: *Mirroring and Striping*

Table 4.1 shows how Oracle suggests RAID should be used with Oracle database files.

RAID	TYPE OF RAID	CONTROL FILE	DATA-BASE FILE	REDO LOG FILE	ARCHIVE LOG FILE
0	Striping	Avoid	OK	Avoid	Avoid
1	Shadowing	Best	OK	Best	Best
0+1	Striping and Shadowing	OK	Best	Avoid	Avoid

RAID	TYPE OF RAID	CONTROL FILE	DATA-BASE FILE	REDO LOG FILE	ARCHIVE LOG FILE
3	Striping with static parity	OK	OK	Avoid	Avoid
5	Striping with rotating parity	OK	Best if RAID0-1 not available	Avoid	Avoid

Table 4.1: *RAID Recommendations (From Metalink NOTE: 45635.1)*

RAID Setup for SCSI

Properly setup RAID allows much higher performance than just a bunch of disks (JBOD.) For the same volume a RAID 5, RAID 1-0 or RAID 0-1 array delivers a higher IO bandwidth than a JBOD array. However, remember from chapter 3 that only one device can communicate over a SCSI bus at the same time. Therefore, if you have multiple SCSI chains you should strip across chains not along chains. In a SCSI based arrays disks are often arranged in what are known as trays (or sometimes bricks) with each tray of eight disks formed from a single SCSI bus. The buses in the SCSI array are then grouped on the SCSI array backbone, which is usually fibre based (1-2 gigabit/sec capacity.) In addition to the additional command latency issues that would occur if multiple devices in the same chain where striped together, if you stripe along chains you could overload the SCSI bus for MB/sec. Figure 4.4 shows this concept.

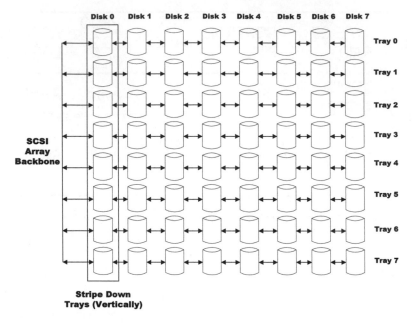

Figure 4.4: *SCSI Array*

Several companies offer pre-built arrays, among them are EMC, Hitachi, Compaq (now HP) and IBM Shark. Let's look at what they have to offer.

EMC Storage Arrays

The EMC Clariion provides a redundant architecture allowing multiple paths to each disk in the array. Figure 4.5 shows this architecture. Notice the two storage processors, mirrored caches, CPU and fibre controllers. This redundancy of components allows multiple paths and high performance. The Clariion ranges from the CX300 to the CX700 series and up to 58.4 terabytes of storage.

Clariion CX200 Block Diagram

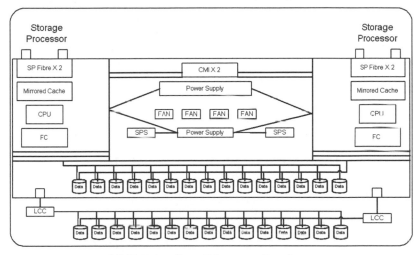

30 Drives Per Storage System

Figure 4.5: *EMC Clariion Architecture.*

Hitachi Storage Arrays

Hitachi offers several versions of its Thunder series arrays the 9200 and the 9900 models. The Thunder arrays offer 1.8 to 83.3 terabytes of storage. As you can see from Figure 4.6, the Hitachi Thunder also incorporates dual components to provide redundancy and high performance.

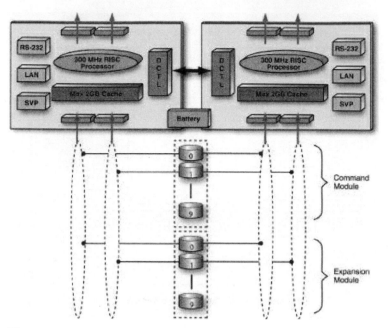

Figure 4.6: *Hitachi Architecture*

Compaq (HP) Storage Arrays

The Compaq (HP) storage arrays range from 3 to 9.1 terabytes of storage for their low-range, up to 70 terabytes in the enterprise range arrays. HP provides a conventional structure with redundant controllers and multiple fibre channel connections using multiple bays of drive enclosures acting as a single array system.

Figure 4.7: *HP Compaq Arrays*

IBM Storage Arrays

IBM offers up to 83.6 terabytes of storage capability in their ESS series arrays. The IBM FAStT array can handle up to 56 terabytes of storage. The general layout of the ESS server is shown in figure 4.8.

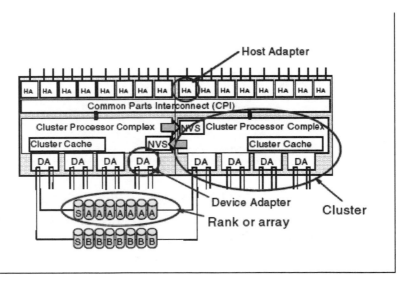

Figure 4.8: *IBM ESS Storage array Schematic*

As you can see from figure 4-7, the ESS array provides the same type of redundant control and data pathing as in the other array solutions.

SUN StorEdge Storage Arrays

The StorEdge technology from SUN allows for up to 417 terabytes of storage in the T3 configuration. The basic structure of the StorEdge array is shown in figure 4.9.

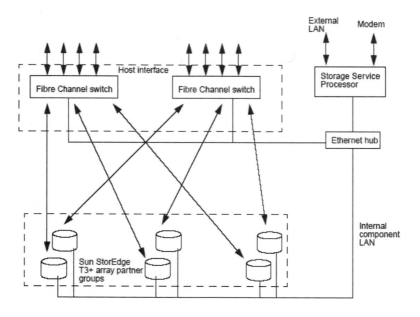

Figure 4.9: *SUN StorEdge Architecture*

As you can see the SUN StorEdge utilizes a single storage service processor so it doesn't have the same redundancy as the other systems at the individual array or brick level. It does provide redundant paths to disks however.

Commonalities between the Arrays

The arrays we have taken a quick look at all have certain things in common:

- They are composed of collections of individual disks.

- They generally use SCSI or Fibre connections.

- They have a controller or controllers that optimize the commands sent from the various hosts.

- They all have caches that optimize common types of read and write activities.

The most critical concepts with the arrays are the ones that govern how they perform read-ahead and write-behind operations. The different systems use different algorithms to accomplish these activities, some are more efficient than others, and which is the best for your environment may be difficult to determine.

Another important aspect is how the data is laid out on the drives in the array. If the drives are not properly configured the array will not perform properly.

Memory Caches

In an effort to improve the IO characteristics of their disks, manufacturers added memory caches to allow read and write caching. Unfortunately, these caches are usually too small to be of much help with database level performance as they are usually a very small fraction of a percent of the total disk capacity. Of what real use is a disk cache of a couple of megabytes on a 200 gigabyte disk holding a database table that is 60 gigabytes in size? The cache soon becomes saturated and any IO benefit is eliminated. Disk array manufacturers such as EMC and Hitachi have also provided larger amounts of cache, in the tens of gigabyte range, which in some situations does help improve IO rates, depending on how efficiently the application uses the data stored in the database. For example, if the application is poorly written and does multiple full scans of multi-gigabyte tables then again the cache becomes saturated and you fall back to disk IO speeds. For that matter, in some environments such as data warehouses and decision support systems, the scanning of large, sometimes hundreds of gigabyte tables, is common place, this can quickly tax even the largest cache systems.

IO Profiles

This all points to the fact that in order to get the maximum performance from your disk system you must understand the IO characteristics (the profile) of your database system, be it Oracle, SQL Server, Informix, UDB or MySQL. You must tune your disk architecture to support the expected IO profile and must tune the database system to take advantage of the disk architecture. For example, an Oracle database has different IO characteristics depending on whether it is reading or writing data and what type of read or write it is doing. Other databases have fixed read/write sizes.

You must determine the IO profile for your database and then use the IO profile of the database to determine the maximum and minimum IO size. The IO profile will tell you what percentage of IO is large IO and what percentage is small IO, it will also give you the expected IO rate in IO/second.

Once you have the IO per second you can determine the IO capacity (number of drives) needed to support your database.

The first rule of tuning your disk system is - size first for IO capacity, then for volume.

Some back of the envelope calculations for the number of spindles needed to support IO rate are:

- RAID10 with active read/write to all mirrors:
- MAX(CEILING(IOR/(NSIOR*M),M),2*M)

Where:

- IOR is expected maximum IO rate in IO/sec
- NSIOR is the average non-sequential IO rate of the disks in IO/sec (range of 90-100 for RAID10)
- M is the number of mirrors

(The maximum of the IO rate divided by the average non-sequential IO rate per disk times the number of mirrors to the nearest power of M or 2*M)

RAID5 assuming 1 parity disk:

- MAX((IOR/CNSIOR)+1,3)

Where:

- IOR is expected maximum IO rate in IO/sec
- CNSIOR is the corrected average non-sequential IO rate of the disks in IO/sec (range of 60-90 for RAID5)

(The maximum of the IO rate divided by the average non-sequential IO rate per disk corrected for RAID5 penalties plus 1 disk for the parity disk)

The correction for the non-sequential IO rate for RAID is due to the up to 400% penalty on writes (writes take 4 times linger than reads on the same drive). In some cases, on RAID5, this can go as high as 6400% (writes take 64 times as long as reads for the same file) when combined with other problems such as fragmentation.

A case in point, early RAID architectures utilized the "stripe shallow and wide" mind set where files where broken into small pieces and spread over a large number of disks. For example, stripe unites per disk of as small as 8K was common. Many systems read in IO sizes of 64K or larger. This means that to satisfy a single IO request 8 disks of the RAID set were required, if there were fewer than 8 disks in the set, disks would have to undergo 2 or more IOs to satisfy the request. This sounds fine if you are talking about a single user wanting to read a large file from a large group of disks very quickly, however, what happens when you have 10 or 100 or 1000 concurrent users all wanting to do the same thing?

Tune for Concurrency

This problem with concurrent access and RAID arrays is one of the most prevailing in the industry. The ubiquitous IO wait is usually the predominant wait event in any database system simply due to the fact that IO to memory is in the nanosecond range while IO to disk is in the millisecond range, when you add in blocked access due to multi-disk IO requests you get a snowball effect that can cripple your IO subsystem.

Array manufacturers have begun to recognize this concurrent access problem and have increased the base stripe unit per disk to 64K, matching the IO unit for many systems. Of course, now systems such as SUN and Windows utilize maximum IO sizes of 1 megabyte or larger, so again the array manufacturers are playing catch up to the server manufacturers.

So what is our second rule of tuning disks? Based on the above information the rule is - Always ensure that the primary

IO size for your database system is matched to the IO size of the disk array system.

Of course, the inverse also holds true:

- Always match the stripe unit per disk to the expected majority IO request from your (database) application.

In the 1990's Paul Chen of the University Of Berkeley computer center published a series of papers on tuning disk array stripe unit's size based on expected concurrency. In these papers by Mr. Chen and his associates, they determined that the IO speed (as measured by average seek time) and IO rate (as measured in megabytes per second) for a disk determined the stripe size for performance in an array even when the number of concurrent accesses is not known. There were three formulae derived from these papers:

For non-RAID5 arrays when concurrency is known:

```
SU = (S*APT*DTR*(CON-1)*1.024)+.5K
```

Where:

- SU - Striping unit per disk
- S - Concurrency slope coefficient ($\sim$.25)
- APT - Average positioning time (milliseconds)
- DTR - Data transfer rate (Megabyte/sec)
- CON - number of concurrent users.
- $1.024 = 1s/1000ms*1024K/1M$ (conversion factors for units)

Therefore, for a drive that has an average seek time of 5.6 ms and a transfer rate of 20 Mbyte/second the calculated stripe unit for a 20 concurrent user base would be:

```
(.25*5.6*20*(19)*1.024)+.5 = 545K (or ~512K)
```

For a system where you didn't know the concurrency, the calculation becomes:

```
SU =(2/3*APT*DTR)
```

So for the same drive:

```
2/3*5.6*20*1.024 = 76.46K so rounding up ~128K or rounding down 64K
```

And, from Chen's final paper, a formula for RAID5 arrays is:

```
0.5*5.6*20*1.024 = 57.34 (rounding up 64K)
```

"Know your formulas! Test on Monday. "

The values for average access time and transfer rate used in these examples is actually fairly low when compared to more advanced drives, so the stripe sizes shown above are probably low by at least a factor of 2 or more. When average seek times drop, the transfer rate increases. For example, on a Ultra3 SCSI 15K drive, the spec for average seek may drop to 4.7 ms, however the transfer rate leaps to 70 Mbyte per second. So, the over all value of the combined factor goes from 112 to 329, a 293% increase.

The IO Path

The other major factor to consider is the ability to transfer the data from the disks to the CPU. This transfer of the data from the disk to the CPU is carried out by the controllers and other interface components. Each controller in a system usually has 2 or more paths to the disk arrays. The more paths to and from the disk array the more data that can be transferred. This leads to the third rule for tuning disk arrays - always plan transfer paths for peak load, not average load.

In one situation, there was a client who switched to a more advanced disk array with faster disks, a new server with faster CPUs and yet the system performed at half the speed of the older system. Investigation showed they had decided to reduce the available disk paths to 2/3 of the previous number (from 12 to 8) based on "average" IO requirements. They soon discovered that while this was fine for day-to-day processing, it spelled real trouble for end-of-month, end-of-quarter and end-of-year processing as well as payday processing.

Make sure IO is spread evenly in a load-balanced methodology not a cascade based methodology across the paths for the controllers. In a load-balanced methodology, the load is spread evenly across all of the paths allocated to a given server. In a cascade methodology, subsequent paths are not utilized until the primary reaches a certain percentage of load.

The 100% Myth

Many system administrators are guilty of perpetuating the 100% myth. This myth states that you don't need more assets (be it disk, CPU, or Memory) until the existing asset is 100% utilized. This leads to performance issues in the area of disks. Due to disk physics the best performance for a disk is at the outer edges, once you get towards the inner sectors performance decreases because of the distance the head must travel to read the data and other factors. In the good old days, administrators spent much time positioning frequently used files on the outer edges of disks.

While physically positioning files on disks is difficult if not impossible in modern RAID systems, you should endeavor not to fill the disks to 100% of capacity. Some experts say don't use more then 30% if you want maximum performance, others 50%. It really depends on how the system is used, the operating system and the RAID array system. For example, the Clariion from EMC promises to tune the placement of files such that frequently used files are in the best locations.

Should I Worry About Fragmentation?

The answer here is it depends. Windows based environments (NT, W2K) are prone to fragmentation due to the opportunistic write algorithm that writes back blocks to the first available sector instead of their original sector. This is even true for the pre-allocated files used by most databases. Another fragmentation prone environment is AIX. And, of course, anyone still using OpenVMS will also know all they ever want to about the costs of fragmentation.

In Windows, AIX and OpenVMS, you will need to monitor for fragmentation and defragement as required. Be sure to verify with your disk array vendor that defragmentation is possible or allowed on their systems. If it becomes severe, you may need to backup the array, rebuild it and then repopulate it to get around specific vendor limitations.

What About Write Caching?

Most RAID adapters have a setting that specifies whether the write cache is set to "write-through" (physically writing the information on disk before acknowledging the write to the operating system) or "write-cache" (providing acknowledgement to the operating system after the data has been cached for write but before it has been physically written to disk). For Oracle, it is recommended that setting this parameter to write-through is good practice. What would happen if a power outage occurs after the write acknowledgement is received by the operating system (and the database instance) but before the data is written to disk? Obviously, a datafile error will be encountered on the next startup of the instance due to the missing write. More and more RAID adapters overcome this problem by battery backup of the cache contents. In this case, even if the power fails, the contents of the cache that is not written to disk will be maintained by the battery until the power is restored and the server hardware restarted. However, make sure the batteries are changed at the proper frequency.

If this feature is used to provide better write performance, then its resilience should be thoroughly tested prior to placing a database server configured with write-cache settings into production use. If the write-cache setting does not absolutely guarantee protection from data loss, do not use it. Check with your specific hardware vendor for detailed information regarding the functionality of the selected array controllers and their specific settings.

Conclusion

Now that we have taken a good look at disk striping, shadowing, mirroring as well as the different aspects of disk arrays, we'll move on to disk monitoring in the next chapter.

References

Peter M. Chen and David A. Patterson. *Maximizing Performance in a Striped Disk Array.* In Proceedings of the 1990 InternationalSymposium on Computer Architecture, pages 322–331, May 1990.

Peter M. Chen and Edward K. Lee, *Striping in a RAID Level 5 Disk Array.* Proceedings of the 1995 ACM SIGMETRICS Conference on Measurement and Modeling of Computer Systems

Drew Rob. *Hard Disks And How They Are Organized.* Enterprise Operations Management, Aurbach Publications, *CRC Press, 2003.*

Disk Monitoring

Introduction

Monitoring disk performance is getting more and more difficult with each improvement to disk technology. In the days when we ran single disks and spread our files across them, it was easy to pinpoint the location of the hot drives we needed to fix. Now with striping, plaiding and other even more esoteric technologies, without resorting to the vendor supplied tools, it can be nearly impossible to track a single hot disk.

"Just how hot is a hot disk?"

However, is it really important to find a "hot" disk? Unless you are running in single disk sets (jbod technology) then knowing a hot disk isn't quite as important. However, we are still interested in disk performance and tracking data file and other IO involved in our databases. The database administrator and system manager must still monitor IO, either through Oracle, through the OS or via performance monitoring tools provided by the disk array or storage system software vendors such as Veritas.

Let's look at the different options that are available. First, we will look at what is available in Oracle, then we will look at OS tools.

Oracle Monitoring

When you use Oracle monitoring, at least in 9i and lower versions, you were somewhat limited in what monitoring you could perform. You could capture total IO since startup, IO/second since startup, and could get this information on a per datafile or tempfile basis. The *v$filestat* and *v$tempstat* dynamic performance views provide the IO statistics from Oracle's point of view. The views inside Oracle cannot see any non-Oracle related IO. In an Oracle Real Applications cluster, the GV versions of these views must be used to see the full IO profile. *Fileio.sql* listed below shows an example select statement to generate both regular and temporary file IO.

🖫 **Fileio.sql**

```
-- *****************************************************
-- Copyright © 2003 by Rampant TechPress
-- This script is free for non-commercial purposes
-- with no warranties.  Use at your own risk.
--
-- To license this script for a commercial purpose,
-- contact info@rampant.cc
-- *****************************************************
rem
rem NAME: fileio.sql
rem
rem FUNCTION: Reports on the file io status of all of the
rem FUNCTION: datafiles in the database.
```

```
rem HISTORY:
rem WHO             WHAT          WHEN
rem Mike Ault                     Created        1/5/96
rem
column sum_io1 new_value st1 noprint
column sum_io2 new_value st2 noprint
column sum_io new_value divide_by noprint
column Percent format 999.999 heading 'Percent|Of IO'
column brratio format 999.99 heading 'Block|Read|Ratio'
column bwratio format 999.99 heading 'Block|Write|Ratio'
column phyrds heading 'Physical | Reads'
column phywrts heading 'Physical | Writes'
column phyblkrd heading 'Physical|Block|Reads'
column phyblkwrt heading 'Physical|Block|Writes'
column name format a45 heading 'File|Name'
column file# format 9999 heading 'File'
column dt new_value today noprint
select to_char(sysdate,'ddmonyyyyhh24miss') dt from dual;
set feedback off verify off lines 132 pages 60 sqlbl on trims on
rem
select
    nvl(sum(a.phyrds+a.phywrts),0) sum_io1
from
    sys.v_$filestat a;
select nvl(sum(b.phyrds+b.phywrts),0) sum_io2
from
       sys.v_$tempstat b;
select &st1+&st2 sum_io from dual;
rem
@title132 'File IO Statistics Report'
spool rep_out\&db\fileio&&today
select
    a.file#,b.name, a.phyrds, a.phywrts,
    (100*(a.phyrds+a.phywrts)/&divide_by) Percent,
    a.phyblkrd, a.phyblkwrt, (a.phyblkrd/greatest(a.phyrds,1))
brratio,
     (a.phyblkwrt/greatest(a.phywrts,1)) bwratio
from
    sys.v_$filestat a, sys.v_$dbfile b
where
    a.file#=b.file#
union
select
    c.file#,d.name, c.phyrds, c.phywrts,
    (100*(c.phyrds+c.phywrts)/&divide_by) Percent,
    c.phyblkrd, c.phyblkwrt,(c.phyblkrd/greatest(c.phyrds,1))
brratio,
     (c.phyblkwrt/greatest(c.phywrts,1)) bwratio
from
    sys.v_$tempstat c, sys.v_$tempfile d
where
    c.file#=d.file#
order by
    1
/
spool off
pause Press enter to continue
```

```
set feedback on verify on lines 80 pages 22
clear columns
ttitle off
```

The output from the above script is shown below.

```
Date: 11/09/03
Page:   1
Time: 01:24 PM                                          File IO
Statistics Report                                       PERFSTAT
                                                          testdb

database


Physical   Physical   Block    Block
   File                                        Physical
Physical   Percent        Block       Block     Read   Write
 File Name                                                Reads
Writes    Of IO     Reads     Writes   Ratio   Ratio
-----  -------------------------------  -----------  ----------  -----
-----  --------  ----------  ----------  -------  ------
      1 /data001/oradata/testdb/system01.dbf                     27396
2992   53.526       55735        2992    2.03    1.00
      1 /data001/oradata/testdb/temp01.dbf                        1703
1357    5.390        7184        7177    4.22    5.29
      2 /data001/oradata/testdb/undotbs01.dbf                      151
18034  32.032         151       18034    1.00    1.00
      3 /data001/oradata/testdb/drsys01.dbf                        116
107     .393         116         107    1.00    1.00
      4 /data001/oradata/testdb/indx01.dbf                         117
107     .395         117         107    1.00    1.00
      5 /data001/oradata/testdb/tools01.dbf                        890
1403    4.039        1137        1403    1.28    1.00
      6 /data001/oradata/testdb/users01.dbf                        115
107     .391         115         107    1.00    1.00
      7 /data001/oradata/testdb/xdb01.dbf                          183
107     .511         194         107    1.06    1.00
      8 /data001/oradata/testdb/olof_data01.dbf                   1045
620    2.933        1242         620    1.19    1.00
      9 /data001/oradata/testdb/olof_idx01.dbf                     116
107     .393         116         107    1.00    1.00
```

Another important measurement is the actual timing. You should note that on some systems and some disk subsystems the IO timing data can be bogus, so always compare it against actual *iostat* numbers. An example IO timing report is shown below.

```
Date: 11/21/03
Page:   1
```

```
     FILE# NAME
PHYRDS    PHYWRTS READTIM/PHYRDS WRITETIM/PHYWRTS
---------- ------------------------------------------------------------
- ---------- ---------- -------------- ----------------
        5 /oracle/oradata/testdb/tools01_01.dbf
318        153      .377358491      .150326797
        1 /oracle/oradata/testdb/system01.dbf
3749       806      .332622033        2.3101737
        9 /oracle/oradata/testdb/tcmd_data01_03.dbf
442389     1575     .058064283        6.90095238
        8 /oracle/oradata/testdb/tcmd_data01_02.dbf
540596     2508     .057647485        5.11961722
        7 /oracle/oradata/testdb/tcmd_data01_01.dbf
14446868   1177     .036516842        2.62531861
       10 /oracle/oradata/testdb/tcmd_idx01_02.dbf
15694      5342     .035746145        6.50074878
        3 /oracle/oradata/testdb/rbs01_01.dbf
757        25451    .034346103       10.7960002
       11 /oracle/oradata/testdb/tcmd_data01_04.dbf
1391       606      .023005032        6.66336634
        6 /oracle/oradata/testdb/tcmd_idx01_01.dbf
1148402    10220    .015289942        6.35831703
        2 /oracle/oradata/testdb/temp01_01.dbf
34961      8835     0                0
        4 /oracle/oradata/testdb/users01_01.dbf
78         76       0                0

11 rows selected.
```

The output in listing above shows that all of our IO timing is at or below 10 milliseconds. Normally, we would consider this to be a good performance for disks, however, most modern arrays can give sub-millisecond response times by use of caching and by spreading IO across multiple platters. While many "experts" say anything less than 10-20 milliseconds is good, that was based on old disk technology. If your disk system isn't giving response times that are at 5 milliseconds or less then you need to look at tuning the IO subsystems.

Another interesting statistic is the overall IO rate for the system as it relates to Oracle. This is easily calculated using PL/SQL as is shown below.

```
-- ****************************************************
-- Copyright © 2003 by Rampant TechPress
-- This script is free for non-commercial purposes
-- with no warranties.  Use at your own risk.
--
-- To license this script for a commercial purpose,
-- contact info@rampant.cc
-- ****************************************************
set serveroutput on
declare
cursor get_io is select
        nvl(sum(a.phyrds+a.phywrts),0) sum_io1,to_number(null)
sum_io2
from sys.gv_$filestat a
union
select
        to_number(null) sum_io1, nvl(sum(b.phyrds+b.phywrts),0)
sum_io2
from
        sys.gv_$tempstat b;
now date;
elapsed_seconds number;
sum_io1 number;
sum_io2 number;
sum_io12 number;
sum_io22 number;
tot_io number;
tot_io_per_sec number;
fixed_io_per_sec number;
temp_io_per_sec number;
begin
open get_io;
for i in 1..2 loop
fetch get_io into sum_io1, sum_io2;
if i = 1 then sum_io12:=sum_io1;
else
sum_io22:=sum_io2;
end if;
end loop;
select sum_io12+sum_io22 into tot_io from dual;
select sysdate into now from dual;
select ceil((now-max(startup_time))*(60*60*24)) into elapsed_seconds
from gv$instance;
fixed_io_per_sec:=sum_io12/elapsed_seconds;
temp_io_per_sec:=sum_io22/elapsed_seconds;
tot_io_per_sec:=tot_io/elapsed_seconds;
dbms_output.put_line('Elapsed Sec :'||to_char(elapsed_seconds,
'9,999,999.99'));
dbms_output.put_line('Fixed
IO/SEC:'||to_char(fixed_io_per_sec,'9,999,999.99'));
dbms_output.put_line('Temp IO/SEC :'||to_char(temp_io_per_sec,
'9,999,999.99'));
```

```
dbms_output.put_line('Total IO/SEC:'||to_char(tot_io_Per_Sec,
'9,999,999.99'));
end;
/
```

An example of the output from this report is shown below.

```
SQL> @io_sec
Elapsed Sec :    43,492.00
Fixed IO/SEC:       588.33
Temp IO/SEC :        95.01
Total IO/SEC:       683.34

PL/SQL procedure successfully executed
```

By examining the total average IO/SEC for the database, we can determine if our IO subsystem is capable of handling the load. For example, if the above listing was for a RAID 10 system with 10 disks in an 5 way stripe in a 2 way mirror array, then we know we don't have any problems with IO rate (10 DISKS * 110 IO/SEC/DISK = ~1100 IO/SEC max rate). However, if we only have 6 disks in a RAID5, then we probably are having periods when IO is saturated (5 DISKS * 90 IO/SEC/DISK = ~ 450 IO/SEC max rate). Remember that the above IO rate is an average, this means that if we have an equal distribution about the mean, then 50% of the time the IO rate was *higher* than this reported value of 683 IO/SEC.

The other indications of possible IO related problems with Oracle are examination of IO related wait events from the wait interface of the Oracle kernel. If your statspack reports, or home-grown reports show that any of the following waits are the majority wait on your system, then look at tuning the IO system in relationship to Oracle:

- Db file sequential read – An event generated during index and other short term read events.

- Db file scattered read – An event generated during full table and index scans.

- Db file parallel write – An event generated during writes to multiple extents across multiple datafiles.

- Log file or control file writes – Events generated during waits to write to a log or control file.

- Direct path read or write – Events generated during hash, sort, global temporary table IO or other direct operations.

- LGWR waits – Events generated during writes to the redo logs.

You must look at these events in relationship to their overall contribution to the total service time. For an example, look at Figure 5.1.

```
Date: 02/03/04
Page:   1
Time: 08:31 AM                                  System
Events Percent                                  MAULT
                                                   testdb
database


Percent    Percent
                                     Total      Average
Of  of Total
Event Name                           Waits      Waits  Time
Waited Non-Idle Waits    Uptime
------------------------------- ------------ ------------ -----------
- --------------- ---------
CPU used when call started              0          0
3,580,091       52.659   3.8499
db file sequential read         9,434,983          0
1,278,929       18.811   1.3753
enqueue                               302      2,899
875,552         12.878   .9415
wait for stopper event to be i      1,526        194
295,860          4.352   .3182
ncreased

db file scattered read            430,041          1
261,103          3.841   .2808
log file parallel write               339        590
199,881          2.940   .2149
db file parallel write             32,240          5
170,070          2.502   .1829
```

```
...                                                      ----------
--
sum
6,798,684
```

Figure 5.1: *Example Wait Report In Comparison to CPU Time*

So even if we eliminated all IO related wait times in the above report, we would only reduce our service time by about 27%. Don't always assume fixing IO will give large performance returns. If you have CPU usage issues (Logical, rather than Physical IO), adding the fastest disks in the world may not help your performance that much. This directs us to the major tuning point for any Oracle or other database system: Tune the code first! Make your SQL as optimized as possible for both Logical and Physical IO, then tackle other issues.

In his excellent whitepaper on tuning Logical verses Physical IO, *Why You Should Focus on LIOs Instead of PIOs,* Cary Millsap of Hotsos Enterprises Inc., gives compelling evidence that you should perhaps concentrate on LIO reduction and then PIO will take care of itself.

The report in Figure 5.1 was generated using the following script.

🖫 **wait_report**

```
-- ***************************************************
-- Copyright © 2003 by Rampant TechPress
-- This script is free for non-commercial purposes
-- with no warranties.  Use at your own risk.
--
-- To license this script for a commercial purpose,
-- contact info@rampant.cc
-- ***************************************************

col event format a30 heading 'Event Name'
col waits format 999,999,999 heading 'Total|Waits'
col average_wait format 999,999,999 heading 'Average|Waits'
col time_waited format 999,999,999 heading 'Time Waited'
col total_time new_value divide_by noprint
```

```
col value new_value val noprint
col percent format 999.990 heading 'Percent|Of|Non-Idle Waits'
col duration new_value millisec noprint
col p_of_total heading 'Percent|of Total|Uptime' format 999.9999
set lines 132 feedback off verify off pages 50
 select to_number(sysdate-startup_time)*86400*1000 duration from
v$instance;
select
sum(time_waited) total_time
from v$system_event
where total_waits-total_timeouts>0
    and event not like 'SQL*Net%'
    and event not like 'smon%'
    and event not like 'pmon%'
    and event not like 'rdbms%'
        and event not like 'PX%'
        and event not like 'sbt%'
        and event not in ('gcs remote message','ges remote
message','virtual circuit status','dispatcher timer') ;
select value from v$sysstat where name ='CPU used when call
started';
@title132 'System Events Percent'
break on report
compute sum of time_waited on report
spool rep_out/&db/sys_events
select name event,
        0 waits,
  0 average_wait,
  value time_waited,
  value/(&&divide_by+&&val)*100 Percent,
  value/&&millisec*100 p_of_total
from v$sysstat
where name ='CPU used when call started'
union
select event,
      total_waits-total_timeouts waits,
      time_waited/(total_waits-total_timeouts) average_wait,
      time_waited,
      time_waited/(&&divide_by+&&val)*100 Percent,
      time_waited/&&millisec*100 P_of_total
from v$system_event
where total_waits-total_timeouts>0
    and event not like 'SQL*Net%'
    and event not like 'smon%'
    and event not like 'pmon%'
    and event not like 'rdbms%'
        and event not like 'PX%'
        and event not like 'sbt%'
        and event not in ('gcs remote message','ges remote
message','virtual circuit status','dispatcher timer')
        and time_waited>0
order by percent desc
/
spool off
clear columns
ttitle off
```

```
clear computes
clear breaks
```

Now, let's examine the use of operating system level commands to monitor disks in UNIX and Linux.

Operating System Monitoring of Disks

One free UNIX utility is very valuable for identifying disk I/O bottlenecks. This utility is *iostat* and it is shipped as a standard with almost every release of UNIX and Linux. The Linux MAN page for the *iostat* command shows that there are numerous options. See below

---

IOSTAT(1)   Linux User's Manual   IOSTAT(1)

NAME

    iostat - Report Central Processing Unit (CPU) statistics and input/output statistics for devices and partitions.

SYNOPSIS

    iostat [-c | -d] [-k] [-t] [-V] [-x [device]] [interval [count]]

DESCRIPTION

The iostat command is used for monitoring system input/output device loading by observing the time the devices are active in relation to their average transfer rates. The iostat command generates reports that can be used to change system configuration to better balance the input/output load between physical disks.

The first report generated by the iostat command provides statistics concerning the interval of time since the system was booted. Each subsequent report covers the time since the previous report. All statistics are reported each time the iostat command is run. The report consists of a CPU header row followed by a row of CPU statistics. On multiprocessor systems, CPU statistics are

---

calculated system-wide as averages among all processors. A device header row is displayed followed by a line of statistics for each device that is configured.

The interval parameter specifies the amount of time in seconds between each report. The first report contains statistics for the time since system startup (boot). Each subsequent report contains statistics collected during the interval since the previous report. The count parameter can be specified in conjunction with the interval parameter. If the count parameter is specified, the value of count determines the number of reports generated at interval seconds apart. If the interval parameter is specified without the count parameter, the iostat command generates reports continuously.

REPORTS

The iostat command generates two types of reports, the CPU Utilization report and the Device Utilization report.

CPU Utilization Report

The first report generated by the iostat command is the CPU Utilization Report. For multiprocessor systems, the CPU values are global averages among all processors. The report has the following format:

%user - Show the percentage of CPU utilization that occurred while executing at the user level (application).

%nice - Show the percentage of CPU utilization that occurred while executing at the user level with nice priority.

%sys - Show the percentage of CPU utilization that occurred while executing at the system level (kernel).

%idle - Show the percentage of time that the CPU or CPUs were idle.

Device Utilization Report

The second report generated by the iostat command is the Device Utilization Report. The device report provides statistics on a per physical device or partition basis. The report may show the following fields, depending on whether -x and -k options are used or not:

Device: - This column gives the device name, which is displayed as hdiskn with 2.2 kernels, for the nth device. It is displayed as devm-n with newer kernels, where m is the major number of the device, and n a distinctive number. When the -x option is used, the device name as listed in the /dev directory is displayed.

tps - Indicates the number of transfers per second that were issued to the device. A transfer is an I/O request to the device. Multiple logical requests can be combined into a single I/O request to the device. A transfer is of indeterminate size.

Blk_read/s - Indicate the amount of data read from the drive expressed in a number of blocks per second. Blocks are equivalent to sectors with post 2.4 kernels and therefore have a size of 512 bytes. With older kernels, a block is of indeterminate size.

Blk_wrtn/s - Indicates the amount of data written to the drive expressed in a number of blocks per second.

Blk_read - The total number of blocks read.

Blk_wrtn - The total number of blocks written.

kB_read/s - Indicates the amount of data read from the drive expressed in kilobytes per second. Data displayed are valid only with kernels 2.4 and later.

kB_wrtn/s - Indicates the amount of data written to the drive expressed in kilobytes per second. Data displayed are valid only with kernels 2.4 and later.

kB_read - The total number of kilobytes read. Data displayed are valid only with kernels 2.4 and later.

kB_wrtn - The total number of kilobytes written. Data displayed are valid only with kernels 2.4 and later.

rqm/s - The number of read requests merged per second that were issued to the device.

wrqm/s - The number of write requests merged per second that were issued to the device.

r/s - The number of read requests that were issued to the device per second.

w/s - The number of write requests that were issued to the device per second.

rsec/s - The number of sectors read from the device per second.

wsec/s - The number of sectors written to the device per second.

rkB/s - The number of kilobytes read from the device per second.

wkB/s - The number of kilobytes written to the device per second.

avgrq-sz - The average size (in sectors) of the requests that were issued to the device.

avgqu-sz - The average queue length of the requests that were issued to the device.

await - The average time (in milliseconds) for I/O requests issued to the device to be served.

svctm - The average service time (in milliseconds) for I/O requests that were issued to the device.

%util – The percentage of CPU time during which I/O requests were issued to the device.

OPTIONS

-c   The -c option is exclusive of the -d option and displays only the cpu usage report.

-d   The -d option is exclusive of the -c option and displays only the device utilization report.

-k   The Displayed statistics are in kilobytes per second instead of blocks per second. Data displayed are valid only with kernels 2.4 and later.

-t   Print the time for each report displayed.

-V   Print version number and usage then exit.

-x device - Display extended statistics. If no device is given on the command line, then extended statistics are displayed for every device registered in the /proc/partitions file. Please note that Linux kernel needs to be patched for this option to work.

ENVIRONENT

The iostat command takes into account the following environment variable:

S_TIME_FORMAT - If this variable   exists and its value is ISO then the current locale will be ignored when printing the date in the report header. The iostat command will use the ISO format (YYYY-MM-DD) instead.

EXAMPLES:

iostat

Display a single history since boot report for all CPU and Devices.

iostat –d 2

Display a continuous device report at two second intervals.

iostat –d 2 6

Display six reports at two second intervals for all devices.

BUGS

/proc filesystem must be mounted for iostat to work.

FILE

/proc/stat contains system statisitics.

/proc/partitions contains statistics for the devices.

AUTHOR

Sebastien Godard <sebastien.godard@wanadoo.fr>

| Linux | JANUARY 2002 | IOSTAT(1) |

Here is an example of the iostat command on a Linux system:

```
[oracle@aultlinux3 oracle]$ iostat 15
```

When you issue "iostat 15" what you are telling the OS to do is to display one line of output 'for every disk that we have attached to our server. For a setting of 15, we get output every 15 seconds, each showing the amount of I/O for each disk (well, in this case each LUN on device 8, which for my setup, corresponds to a single disk).

A sample of the output follows.

```
Linux 2.4.22-1.2115.nptlsmp (aultlinux3)        04/25/04

avg-cpu:  %user   %nice    %sys   %idle
           0.19    0.05    0.16   99.60

Device:            tps   Blk_read/s   Blk_wrtn/s   Blk_read   Blk_wrtn
dev8-0            1.95        12.52        24.61     988736    1943550
dev8-1           11.24        44.89         0.00    3545052          0
dev8-2            0.00         0.01         0.00       1096          0
dev8-3            0.00         0.01         0.00       1096          0
dev8-4            0.00         0.01         0.00       1096          0
dev8-5            0.00         0.01         0.00       1096          0
dev8-6            0.00         0.01         0.00       1096          0

avg-cpu:  %user   %nice    %sys   %idle
           1.67    0.00    0.23   98.10

Device:            tps   Blk_read/s   Blk_wrtn/s   Blk_read   Blk_wrtn
dev8-0            5.87         0.00       141.33          0       2120
dev8-1           35.00       142.80         0.00       2142          0
dev8-2            0.00         0.00         0.00          0          0
```

```
dev8-3           0.00          0.00          0.00          0          0
dev8-4           0.00          0.00          0.00          0          0
dev8-5           0.00          0.00          0.00          0          0
dev8-6           0.00          0.00          0.00          0          0

avg-cpu:  %user   %nice    %sys   %idle
           0.10    0.00    0.07   99.83

Device:            tps   Blk_read/s   Blk_wrtn/s   Blk_read   Blk_wrtn
dev8-0           1.27          0.00         30.93          0        464
dev8-1          35.00        142.80          0.00       2142          0
dev8-2           0.00          0.00          0.00          0          0
dev8-3           0.00          0.00          0.00          0          0
dev8-4           0.00          0.00          0.00          0          0
dev8-5           0.00          0.00          0.00          0          0
dev8-6           0.00          0.00          0.00          0          0
```

Device 8-0 is the system SATA drive, the other 6 drives are 10k RPM-9.1 gigabyte SCSI disks in a Compaq Storage System U2 array. Right now, the only activity is an attempted start of the cluster ready services for a 10g RAC cluster.

The columns that are sent out in response to the utility execution will depend on the system you execute the command against. In Linux, the basic columns are fairly easy to understand. We have:

- Tps – Transactions per second for the drive, this corresponds to the I/O per seconf for the drive (multiple blocks can take part in each IO operation).

- Blk_read/s – Number of blocks read in a second for this drive.

- Blk_wrtn/s – Number of blocks written in a second for the drive.

- Blk_read and Block_wrtn – total blocks read and written during the time interval.

For SUN, here are the Solaris specific descriptions for the columns:

- % tm_act: The percentage of time that the disk was physically active.

- Kbps: The number of Kbytes transferred per second.

- Tps: the number of I/O requests to the disk.

   (Note that multiple logical I/O requests may be merged into a single physical request.)

- Kb_read: The number of Kbytes read during the interval.

- Kb_wrtn: The number of Kbytes written during the time interval.

- The "% tm_act" shows the percentage of active time for the disk, and this output, when used in conjunction with a statspack report in Oracle 9i and above, can help to show you disk bottlenecks.

Another useful UNIX/Linux utility is *vmstat*. The *vmstat* utility is used to look at virtual memory statistics and provides information on swapping, buffer usage, IO and CPU usage. The Linux MAN page for *vmstat* is shown below.

VMSTAT(8)   Linux User's Manual   VMSTAT(8)

NAME

vmstat - display virtual memory statistics

SYNOPSIS

vmstat [flags] [delay [count]]

DESCRIPTION

The VMSTAT(8) utility reports statistical information about process status, memory consumption, paging activity, block I/O operations, interrupts, context switches, and processor usage.

The VMSTAT(8) utility is most commonly used to produce a continuous report every <u>delay</u> value of seconds. In this mode, the first report given is the average of the statistics since system boot. Each subsequent line pertains to that sampling period (that is, the last <u>delay</u> seconds). If no <u>delay</u> value is given, only one report is given, which is the average since system boot.

The optional <u>count</u> value specifies a maximum number of reports to print before terminating. By default (that is, when no <u>count</u> value is given) vmstat(8) will continue to print reports every <u>delay</u> seconds until interrupted.

OPTIONS

Normal invocation of vmstat(8) does not require any options. The output, however, can be fine-tuned by specifying one or more of the following flags:

--active, -a

Display active and inactive memory statistics in lieu of the buffer and cache statistics.

--noheaders, -n

Do not regularly update the header describing each column. Normally, the header is periodically reprinted to ensure it is always viewable.

--bytes, -b

Display the statistics in bytes.

--kb, -kb

Display the statistics in kilobytes. This is the default.

--mb, -m

Display the statistics in megabytes.

--gb, -g

Display the statistics in gigabytes. Note that the translation silently rounds down any underflow and displays the result as an integer. This means that the translation is efficient and simple, but that a large unit (i.e., MB or GB) with small statistics will display zero and not a decimal fraction.

--version, -V

Display version information and then exit.

--help

Display usage information and then exit.

FIELDS

PROOCS

r: The number of runnable processes (that is, processes running or waiting to run).

b: The number of processes in uninterruptible sleep.

MEMORY

swpd : the amount of memory paged to disk (in KB by default)

free : the amount of free physical memory (in KB by default)

buff : the amount of memory consumed by buffers (in KB by default)

inact : the amount of memory on the inactive list (in KB by default)

active: the amount of memory on the active list (in KB by default)

SWAP

si: the amount of memory paged in from disk (in KB/s by default)

so: the amount of memory paged out to disk (in KB/s by default)

IO

bi: blocks sent out to a block device (in blocks/s)

bo: blocks received from a block device (in blocks/s)

SYSTEM

in: the number of interrupts received (in interrupts/s)

cs: the number of context switches (in switches/s)

CPU

us: percentage of total processor time consumed by user-space

sy: percentage of total processor time consumed by the kernel

wa: percentage of total processor time spent in I/O wait

id: percentage of total processor time spent idle

NOTES

The current implementation of vmstat(8) does not display the traditional "w" field under "procs". This is because Linux is a demand paging operating system and does not support the notion of swapping out entire processes. Thus this statistic is worthless. Older versions of vmstat(8) just displayed a hardcoded zero for this value. Even older versions calculated the field based on the number of RSS pages the process owns. Although this is a close analogy to the concept of "swapped out", it is still a misleading statistic as the Linux kernel has not explicitly decided to swap to disk the entire process.

This version of vmstat(8) displays I/O wait statistics as "wa" under the "cpu" section. This field is not part of traditional vmstat(8) implementations, but Linux kernels since 2.5 have exported this (very useful) information. Earlier kernels will simply display zero for this field.

FILES

/proc/meminfo -- memory information

/proc/stat -- system statistics

/proc/(1-9)*/stat -- process statistics

AUTHORS

Written by Robert Love.

The procps package is maintained by Robert Love and was created by Michael Johnson.

Send bug reports to <procps-list@redhat.com>.

A Linux *vmstat* example run with no load is shown below.

```
[oracle@aultlinux3 oracle]$ vmstat --kb 1 8
procs                memory      swap        io     system         cpu
 r  b  swpd    free   buff  cache  si  so   bi  bo   in   cs us sy wa id
 0  0     0 1105748 183828 366576   0   0   15   6   63   68  0  0  0 100
 0  0     0 1105732 183828 366576   0   0    0  36  119   62  0  0  0 100
 0  1     0 1105728 183828 366576   0   0   65   0  165  300  0  0  0 100
 0  0     0 1105696 103828 366576   0   0   88  28  140  214  0  0  0 100
 0  0     0 1105696 183828 366576   0   0    0   0  113   78  0  0  0 100
 1  0     0 1105728 183828 366576   0   0    0   0  114   70  0  0  0 100
 0  0     0 1105728 183828 366576   0   0    0   0  113   56  0  0  0 100
 0  0     0 1105728 183828 366576   0   0    0   0  114   50  0  0  0 100
```

A run under the same type of load as the *iostat* command in the previous section is shown below.

```
[oracle@aultlinux3 oracle]$ vmstat --kb 5 8
procs                memory      swap        io     system         cpu
 r  b swpd    free   buff  cache  si  so   bi   bo   in   cs us sy wa id
 0  1    0 1101048 183828 366608   0   0   15    6   63   68  0  0  0 100
 0  0    0 1101140 183828 366608   0   0   61   22  142  213  0  0  0 100
 0  0    0 1101120 183828 366608   0   0   92   22  158  289  0  0  0 100
 0  0    0 1101072 183828 366608   0   0   92    8  157  266  0  0  0 100
 0  0    0 1101108 183828 366608   0   0   31   17  129  149  0  0  0 100
 0  0    0 1101088 183828 366608   0   0   92   17  159  288  0  0  0 100
 0  0    0 1101056 183828 366608   0   0   61   14  142  223  0  0  0 100
 0  0    0 1101068 183828 366608   0   0   61   16  142  205  0  0  0 100
```

Of course, just looking at raw *iostat* and *vmstat* numbers doesn't tell you much. You must correlate this information with the data obtained from inside the Oracle database. This is easiest done by utilizing the Oracle statspack package and collecting concurrent statistics between the database and the disk IO subsystem. Donald K. Burleson, in *"High Performance Tuning Using Oracle Statspack"*, shows detailed examples of how this process can be automated.

Using just statspack and system utilities holistic data, which tells you the status internal to Oracle and external with the various UNIX and Linux commands, can be gathered and analyzed.

You can access the data collected by statspack with normal scripts such as the *snapfileio.sql* listed below.

💾 **snapfileio.sql**

```
--  *************************************************
--  Copyright © 2003 by Rampant TechPress
--  This script is free for non-commercial purposes
--  with no warranties.  Use at your own risk.
--
--  To license this script for a commercial purpose,
--  contact info@rampant.cc
--  *************************************************


rem
rem NAME: snapfileio.sql
rem
rem FUNCTION: Reports on the file io status of all of the
rem FUNCTION: datafiles in the database for a single snapshot.

rem HISTORY:
rem WHO            WHAT           WHEN
rem Mike Ault              Created        11/19/03
rem
column sum_io1 new_value st1 noprint
column sum_io2 new_value st2 noprint
column sum_io new_value divide_by noprint
column Percent format 999.999 heading 'Percent|Of IO'
column brratio format 999.99 heading 'Block|Read|Ratio'
column bwratio format 999.99 heading 'Block|Write|Ratio'
column phyrds heading 'Physical | Reads'
column phywrts heading 'Physical | Writes'
column phyblkrd heading 'Physical|Block|Reads'
column phyblkwrt heading 'Physical|Block|Writes'
column filename format a45 heading 'File|Name'
column file# format 9999 heading 'File'
set feedback off verify off lines 132 pages 60 sqlbl on trims on
rem
```

```
select
    nvl(sum(a.phyrds+a.phywrts),0) sum_io1
from
    stats$filestatxs a where snap_id=&&snap;
select nvl(sum(b.phyrds+b.phywrts),0) sum_io2
from
        stats$tempstatxs b where snap_id=&&snap;
select &st1+&st2 sum_io from dual;
rem
@title132 'Snap&&snap File IO Statistics Report'
spool rep_out\&db\fileio&&snap
select
    a.filename, a.phyrds, a.phywrts,
    (100*(a.phyrds+a.phywrts)/&divide_by) Percent,
    a.phyblkrd, a.phyblkwrt, (a.phyblkrd/greatest(a.phyrds,1))
brratio,
      (a.phyblkwrt/greatest(a.phywrts,1)) bwratio
from
    stats$filestatxs a
where
    a.snap_id=&&snap
union
select
    c.filename, c.phyrds, c.phywrts,
    (100*(c.phyrds+c.phywrts)/&divide_by) Percent,
    c.phyblkrd, c.phyblkwrt,(c.phyblkrd/greatest(c.phyrds,1))
brratio,
      (c.phyblkwrt/greatest(c.phywrts,1)) bwratio
from
    stats$tempstatxs c
where
    c.snap_id=&&snap
order by
    1
/
spool off
pause Press enter to continue
set feedback on verify on lines 80 pages 22
clear columns
ttitle off
undef snap
```

Of course, a single statspack reading suffers from the same limitations that a single read of the v$ or gv$ dynamic performance views - it only gives us the cumulative data from when the database was started to the time that the snapshot was taken. A better methodology is shown in *snapdeltafileio.sql*.

```
-- ***************************************************
-- Copyright © 2003 by Rampant TechPress
-- This script is free for non-commercial purposes
-- with no warranties.  Use at your own risk.
--
-- To license this script for a commercial purpose,
-- contact info@rampant.cc
-- ***************************************************


rem
rem NAME: snapdeltafileio.sql
rem
rem FUNCTION: Reports on the file io status of all of
rem FUNCTION: the datafiles in the database across
rem FUNCTION: two snapshots.
rem HISTORY:
rem WHO             WHAT          WHEN
rem Mike Ault               Created        11/19/03
rem
column sum_io1 new_value st1 noprint
column sum_io2 new_value st2 noprint
column sum_io new_value divide_by noprint
column Percent format 999.999 heading 'Percent|Of IO'
column brratio format 999.99 heading 'Block|Read|Ratio'
column bwratio format 999.99 heading 'Block|Write|Ratio'
column phyrds heading 'Physical | Reads'
column phywrts heading 'Physical | Writes'
column phyblkrd heading 'Physical|Block|Reads'
column phyblkwrt heading 'Physical|Block|Writes'
column filename format a45 heading 'File|Name'
column file# format 9999 heading 'File'
set feedback off verify off lines 132 pages 60 sqlbl on trims on
rem
select
    nvl(sum((b.phyrds-a.phyrds)+(b.phywrts-a.phywrts)),0) sum_io1
from
    stats$filestatxs a, stats$filestatxs b
where
        a.snap_id=&&first_snap_id and b.snap_id=&&sec_snap_id
        and a.filename=b.filename;
select
    nvl(sum((b.phyrds-a.phyrds)+(b.phywrts-a.phywrts)),0) sum_io2
from
    stats$tempstatxs a, stats$tempstatxs b
where
        a.snap_id=&&first_snap_id and b.snap_id=&&sec_snap_id
        and a.filename=b.filename;
select &st1+&st2 sum_io from dual;
rem
@title132 'Snap &&first_snap_id to &&sec_snap_id File IO Statistics
Report'
spool rep_out\&db\fileio'&&first_snap_id'_to_'&&sec_snap_id'
```

```
select
    a.filename, b.phyrds -a.phyrds phyrds, b.phywrts-a.phywrts
phywrts,
    (100*((b.phyrds-a.phyrds)+(b.phywrts-a.phywrts))/&divide_by)
Percent,
    b.phyblkrd- a.phyblkrd phyblkrd, b.phyblkwrt-a.phyblkwrt
phyblgwrt,
        ((b.phyblkrd-a.phyblkrd)/greatest((b.phyrds-a.phyrds),1))
brratio,
        ((b.phyblkwrt-a.phyblkwrt)/greatest((b.phywrts-
a.phywrts),1)) bwratio
from
    stats$filestatxs a, stats$filestatxs b
where
        a.snap_id=&&first_snap_id and b.snap_id=&&sec_snap_id
        and a.filename=b.filename
union
select
    c.filename, d.phyrds-c.phyrds phyrds, d.phywrts-c.phywrts
phywrts,
    (100*((d.phyrds-c.phyrds)+(d.phywrts-c.phywrts))/&divide_by)
Percent,
    d.phyblkrd-c.phyblkrd phyblkrd, d.phyblkwrt-c.phyblkwrt
phyblgwrt,
        ((d.phyblkrd-c.phyblkrd)/greatest((d.phyrds-c.phyrds),1))
brratio,
        ((d.phyblkwrt-c.phyblkwrt)/greatest((d.phywrts-
c.phywrts),1)) bwratio
from
    stats$tempstatxs c, stats$tempstatxs d
where
        c.snap_id=&&first_snap_id and c.snap_id=&&sec_snap_id
        and c.filename=d.filename
order by
    1
/
spool off
pause Press enter to continue
set feedback on verify on lines 80 pages 22
clear columns
ttitle off
undef first_snap_id
undef sec_snap_id
```

The report in accepts two snapshot ids and then uses them to calculate the delta between the IO readings. This IO delta information is vital to help pinpoint real IO problems for a given time period. Combined with *iostat* and *vmstat* readings from the same time period, you can get a complete picture of the IO profile of your database. A similar technique can be used for IO timing and other useful delta statistics. These scripts and many others are available from www.rampant.cc.

Automating Statistic Collection

We all have better things to do than sit around and run disk performance scripts. Automate the process using scripts and the cron tab in UNIX and Linux. If you do a simple web search using the search tool of your choice, you can find any number of shell, perl and other scripts to monitor using *iostat*, *vmstat* and *sar*. Rather than recreating the wheel, look to the web for examples of scripts, and of course the Donald K. Burleson book "*High Performance Tuning with Statspack*" also provides a plethora of scripts and examples.

Conclusion

Disk and disk array manufacturers are homogenizing disk arrays to the point where they can get IO rates to match the disk capacity. This results in the spread of the IO across many more platters than ever before. This spread of IO is a good thing but it does make tracking IO problems difficult.

By using the monitoring from inside Oracle and the OS provided tools such as *iostat*, *vmstat* and *sar* (or Windows based GUI monitoring), you can usually find the problem areas. Many array and disk management software manufacturers provide monitoring tools for their arrays, which can track IO down to the spindle.

Always be sure that IO is your problem, spending thousands of dollars of tight IO budget to get only a 25% improvement or less in performance is a sure ticket to a new job. Tune Oracle for PIO and LIO first, then throw hardware at it. In a pinch, you can try solid-state disks. However, if you are not IO bound then even solid-state disks won't help you.

Solid State Disk and Oracle Databases

Introduction

We live in a world of constantly improving hardware technology. Yesterday's mainframe is today's PC, and we are seeing unprecedented improvements to the speed and cost of computer hardware. Moore's Law dictates that hardware costs will constantly fall while prices become constantly cheaper (Figure 6.1).

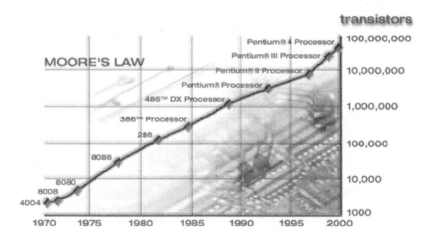

Figure 6.1 - *Moore's Law circa 1975 (Source Intel)*

This rapid change is especially evident for Random Access Memory (RAM). Using RAM memory is critical to the performance of today's database management systems because RAM speed (expressed in nanoseconds) is more then 10,000 times faster than traditional disk storage device speed (expressed in milliseconds). RAM allows data to be accessed much faster than disk technology, and I/O-bound Oracle systems will soon be able to benefit from RAM like never before.

The latest incarnation of RAM storage devices is the solid-state disk (SSD) technology where the ancient spinning platters of magnetic-coated media are replaced with an array of super-fast solid-state RAM. Just as disks were backed-up to tape, today's SSD devices achieve tertiary storage with software mechanisms that write the RAM frames to a back-end disk on the device.

With the cost of SSD at only $1k/gig, many Oracle systems are exploring how to leverage this powerful performance tool for their environment. Smaller database can now run fully-cached with SSD; however, there is debate about the proper use of SSD in an Oracle environment.

Traditional architectures of the 1990's have left us with duplicitous cache areas (web cache, Oracle buffer cache, on-board disk cache), and it has become the challenge of the Oracle DBA to exploit the benefits of SSD for their database application. Let's get started and explore the current state of SSD research.

Oracle Data Caching

Leveraging RAM resources has always been one of the central tasks of the Database Administrator (DBA). By definition, almost all databases are I/O intensive, and minimizing the expensive physical disk I/O has always been a major priority to ensure acceptable performance. Historically, RAM has been a scarce and expensive resource, and the DBA was challenged to find the best "working set" of highly-used data to cache on their precious RAM media.

However, RAM is quite different from other hardware. Unlike CPU speed, which improves every year, RAM speed is constrained by the physics of silicon technology and instead of speed improvements; we see a constant decline in price. CPU speed also continues to outpace RAM speed and this means RAM sub-systems must be localized to keep the CPU's running at full capacity.

In the 1980's, a billion bytes of RAM cost over a million dollars whereas today we can get 1 gigabyte of high-speed RAM storage for less than $1,000. Historically, RAM I/O bandwidth grows one bit every 18 months, making the first decade of the 21st Century the era of 64-bit RAM technology:

- 1970's   8 bit
- 1980's 16 bit
- 1990's 32 bit
- 2000's 64 bit
- 2020's 128 bit

It is clear the dramatic decreases in RAM process are going to change Oracle database architectures. Once a scarce and expensive resource, the Oracle DBA had to spend a huge amount of time managing Oracle memory allocation and optimization. This is about to change.

Today we can buy 100 gigabytes of SSD (i.e., Texas Memory Systems) for about $100,000. By 2007, a gig of RAM is expected to cost the same as a gig of disk today (about $200). Of course, this inexpensive RAM will mean a dramatic change in Oracle database architecture as we abandon the old-fashioned model of disk-based data management in favor of a cache-based approach.

According to David Ensor, Oracle tuning expert, author and Former Oracle Vice President of Oracle Corporation's Performance Group, the increase in CPU power has shifted the bottleneck of many systems to disk I/O.

"Increased server power has meant that disk I/O has replaced CPU power and memory as the limiting factors on throughput for almost all applications and clustering is not a cost-effective way of increasing I/O throughput."

SSD as an Oracle Tuning Tool

The dramatic price-performance ratio of SSD is changing the way that Oracle databases are tuned. Sub-optimal Oracle databases no longer have to undergo expensive and time-consuming re-design, and SSD technology is now competing head-on with Oracle consulting services.

For example, a poorly designed Oracle database might take six-months and over $500,000 in consulting cost to repair. If we use SSD as a remedy, the entire database will run more than ten times faster, within 24 hours, at a fraction of the cost of repairing the source code.

Of course, the code still runs sub-optimally, but the performance complaints are quickly alleviated at a very competitive cost.

As we can see, SSD promises to radically change the way Oracle databases are managed. We must understand the best

---

approach to using this powerful new tool within our Oracle architecture.

RAM Access Speed with Oracle Databases

Now that inexpensive solid-state disk is available, Oracle professionals are struggling to understand how to leverage this new hardware for their databases. Let's start by looking at the nature of Oracle RAM caching and see why this is such an important issue:

- The history of Oracle RAM data buffering

- The problem is duplicitous RAM caches

- The issue of expensive logical I/O

Once we review the existing research, we will be able to gain insights into the best placement for SSD in an Oracle environment.

The History of Oracle RAM Data Buffering

When Oracle was first introduced in the early 1990's, RAM was very expensive and very few databases could afford to run large data buffer regions. Because RAM was such a limited resource, Oracle utilizes a least-frequently-used algorithm within the data buffer to ensure that only the most frequently referenced data remained in the data buffer cache.

As of Oracle10g, we have 7 separate RAM data buffers to hold incoming data blocks. These RAM areas define RAM space for incoming data blocks and are governed by the following Oracle10g parameters. The sum of all of these parameter values determines the total space reserved for Oracle data blocks.

- *db_cache_size*

- *db_keep_cache_size*
- *db_recycle_cache_size*
- *db_2k_cache_size*
- *db_4k_cache_size*
- *db_8k_cache_size*
- *db_16k_cache_size*
- *db_32k_cache_size*

Let's plot the relationship between the size of the RAM data buffers and physical disk reads. In Figure 6.2 we clearly see the non-linear nature of RAM scalability for Oracle.

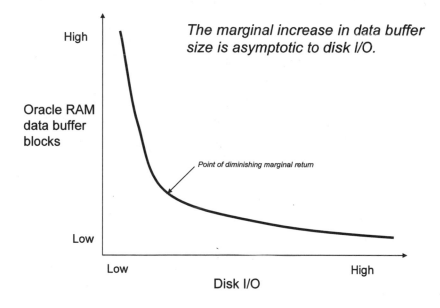

The marginal increase in data buffer size is asymptotic to disk I/O.

High

Oracle RAM data buffer blocks

Point of diminishing marginal return

Low

Low   High

Disk I/O

Figure 6.2 – *The relationship between physical disk I/O and the size of the RAM buffer cache*

This relationship can be expressed mathematically as:

$$\text{RAM Buffer Size} = \frac{n}{\text{Physical reads}}.$$

Where n = an observed constant

This relationship is the basis of the Automatic Memory Management (AMM) features of Oracle10g. Because the Automatic Workload Repository (AWR) is polling the efficiency of the data buffer, The AMM component can compute the point of diminishing marginal returns (in Calculus, the second derivative), and re-assign SGA RAM resources to ensure optimal sizing for all 7 Oracle10g data buffers.

Oracle uses this data to dynamically adjust each of the seven data buffers to keep them at their optimal size. In AMM, Oracle 10g uses the Automated Workload Repository (AWR) to collect historical buffer utilization information and stores the buffer advisory information in the *dba_hist_db_cache_advice* view, and offers a host of *dba_hist* views for Oracle RAM management (Figure 6.3).

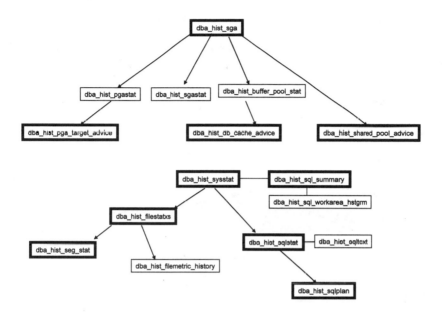

Figure 6.3 – *Oracle10g dba_hist views for Automated Memory Management (AMM)*

When we don't have enough RAM to cache the frequently-used "working set" of data blocks, additional RAM is very valuable.

Figure 6.4 shows how a small increase in RAM results in a large decrease in disk I/O.

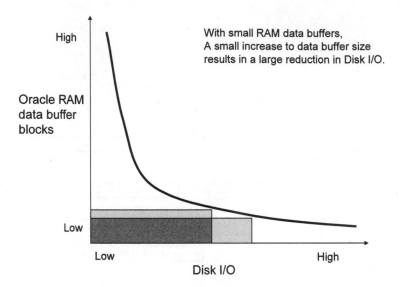

Figure 6.4 – *Too-small data buffers show large marginal reduction of disk I/O*

Traditionally, the optimal size of the Oracle RAM data buffer cache has been the point where the marginal benefit begins to decline, as measured by the acceleration of the curve denoted in Figure 6.2.

However, this marginal benefit does not last forever as shown in Figure 6.5. As we approach full-caching of the Oracle database, it takes a relatively large amount of RAM to reduce physical disk I/O. This is because rarely read data blocks are now being pulled into the SGA data buffers.

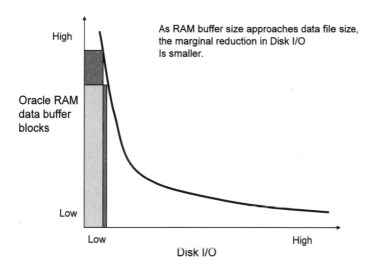

As RAM buffer size approaches data file size, the marginal reduction in Disk I/O Is smaller.

Figure 6.5 – *The diminishing value of RAM buffering as we approach full-caching*

This optimal point is easily calculated with the Oracle10g Automatic Memory Management (AMM) utility. To see how it works, let's step-back and look at the script to display the output from the Oracle *v$db_cache_advice* utility:

💾 cache_advice.sql

```
--    ***************************************************
-- Copyright © 2003 by Rampant TechPress
-- This script is free for non-commercial purposes
-- with no warranties.  Use at your own risk.
--
-- To license this script for a commercial purpose,
-- contact info@rampant.cc
--    ***************************************************
column c1    heading 'Cache Size (m)'          format 999,999,999,999
column c2    heading 'Buffers'                 format 999,999,999
column c3    heading 'Estd Phys|Read Factor'   format 999.90
column c4    heading 'Estd Phys| Reads'        format 999,999,999

select
```

```
   size_for_estimate          c1,
   buffers_for_estimate       c2,
   estd_physical_read_factor  c3,
   estd_physical_reads        c4
from
   v$db_cache_advice
where
   name = 'DEFAULT'
and
   block_size   = (SELECT value FROM V$PARAMETER
                  WHERE name = 'db_block_size')
and
   advice_status = 'ON';
```

When we execute this utility, we can clearly see the relationship between the RAM buffer size and physical reads. In the listing below, note the values range from 10 percent of the current size to double the current size of the *db_cache_size*.

Cache Size (MB)	Buffers	Read Factor	Estd Phys Reads	
30	3,802	18.70	192,317,943	← 10% size
60	7,604	12.83	131,949,536	
91	11,406	7.38	75,865,861	
121	15,208	4.97	51,111,658	
152	19,010	3.64	37,460,786	
182	22,812	2.50	25,668,196	
212	26,614	1.74	17,850,847	
243	30,416	1.33	13,720,149	
273	34,218	1.13	11,583,180	
304	38,020	1.00	10,282,475	Current Size
334	41,822	.93	9,515,878	
364	45,624	.87	8,909,026	
395	49,426	.83	8,495,039	
424	53,228	.79	8,116,496	
456	57,030	.76	7,824,764	
486	60,832	.74	7,563,180	
517	64,634	.71	7,311,729	
547	68,436	.69	7,104,280	
577	72,238	.67	6,895,122	
608	76,040	.66	6,739,731	← 2x size

This predictive model is the basis for Oracle10g AMM. When we take the data from Oracle's predictive mode and plot it, Figure 6.6 shows the tradeoff.

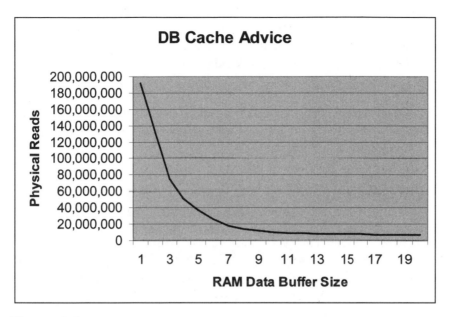

Figure 6.6 – *A plot from the output of v$db_cache_advice*

The main point of this relationship between RAM buffering and physical reads is that all Oracle databases have data that is accessed with differing frequencies. In sum, the larger the working-set of frequently referenced data blocks, the greater the benefit from speeding up block access.

Once we know this, we are in a position to intelligently apply this knowledge to the use of SSD for Oracle.

Allocating Oracle Objects into Multiple RAM Data Buffers

Since very few Oracle database can afford the cost of full RAM caching, many "rules" have developed for the segregation and isolation of cached objects. Some of these "rules of thumb" will give us clues about the best way to utilize SSD in a solid-state Oracle environment:

- Segregate large-table full-table scans - Tables that experience large-table/full-table scans will benefit from the largest supported block size and should be placed in a tablespace with your largest block size.

- Use your RECYCLE Pool - If you are not setting *db_cache_size* to the largest supported block size for your server, you should not use the *db_recycle_cache_size* parameter. Instead, you will want to create a *db_32k_cache_size* (or whatever your max is), and assign all tables that experience frequent large-table/full-table scans to the largest buffer cache in your database.

- Segregate Indexes - in many cases, Oracle SQL statements will retrieve index information via an index range scan, scanning the b-tree or bitmap index for ranges of values that match the SQL search criteria. Hence, it is beneficial to have as much of an index as possible residing in RAM. One of the very first things the Oracle 9i database administrator should do is migrate all of their Oracle indexes into a large blocksize tablespace. Indexes will always favor the largest supported blocksize.

- Segregate random access reads - For those databases that fetch small rows randomly from the disk, the Oracle DBA can segregate these types of tables into 2K Tablespaces. We have to remember that while disk is becoming cheaper every day, we still do not want to waste any available RAM by reading in more information to the RAM number actually going be used by the query. Hence, many Oracle DBAs will use small block size as in cases of tiny, random access record retrieval.

- Segregate LOB column tables - For those Oracle tables that contain raw, long raw, or in-line LOBs, moving the table rows to large block size will have an extremely beneficial effect on disk I/O. Experienced DBAs will check *dba_tables.avg_row_len* to make sure the blocksize is larger than the average size. Row chaining will be reduced while, at the same time, the entire LOB can be read within a single disk I/O, thereby avoiding the additional overhead of having Oracle to go out of read multiple blocks.

- Segregate large-table full-table scan rows - When the recycle pool was first introduced in Oracle8i, the idea was the full table scan data blocks, which are not likely to be re-read by other transactions. They could be quickly flushed through the Oracle SGA, thereby reserving critical RAM for those data blocks that were likely to be re-read by another transaction. In Oracle9i, you can configure your recycle pool to use a smaller block size.

- Check the average row length - The block size for a tables' tablespace should always be greater than the average row length for the table (*dba_tables.avg_row_len*). Note that if it is smaller than the average row length, rows chaining occurs and excessive disk I/O is incurred.

- Use large blocks for data sorting - Your TEMP tablespace will benefit from the largest supported blocksize. This allows disk sorting to happen in large blocks with a minimum of disk I/O.

These suggestions are very important in our examination of the best way to utilize SSD as an alternative caching mechanism.

However, recent TPC-C benchmarks make it clear that very-large RAM regions are a central component in high-performance Oracle databases. The 2004 UNISYS Oracle Windows benchmark exceeded 250,000 transactions per minute using a Windows-based 16-CPU server with 115 gigabytes of Oracle data buffer cache. Here are the Oracle parameters that were used in the benchmark, and we can clearly see the benefit of large-scale RAM caching:

- *db_16k_cache_size* = 15010M

- *db_8k_cache_size* = 1024M

- *db_cache_size*   = 8096M

- *db_keep_cache_size* = 78000M

At this point, it is very clear that RAM resources are a very important factor in maintaining the performance of I/O intensive Oracle systems.

Improving I/O Speed Is Not a Silver Bullet

Please understand that SSD and RAM buffer caching are only important to I/O-intensive Oracle databases. If your Oracle database is constrained by other environmental factors (CPU, network), then speeding-up the I/O sub-system will not result in any appreciable performance gains. To learn about your databases resource bottlenecks, you need only display the top-5 timed events from STATSPACK.

Below is a listing from a typical OLTP database where I/O delay is the main source of wait time. Note that I/O comprises more than 70% of total elapsed time.

```
Top 5 Timed Events
~~~~~~~~~~~~~~~~~~~                                    % Total
Event                              Waits     Time (s)  Ela
Time
--------------------------- ------------ ----------- --------
db file sequential read           2,598     7,146      48.54
db file scattered read           25,519     3,246      22.04
library cache load lock             673     1,363       9.26
CPU time                                    1,154       7.83
log file parallel write          19,157       837       5.68
```

Again, it is critical to note that additional RAM resources may not have any appreciable effect on databases that are not I/O intensive. As shown below, some scientific Oracle databases only read a small set of experimental results and spend the majority of database time performing computations.

```
Top 5 Timed Events
~~~~~~~~~~~~~~~~~                                          % Total
Event                            Waits    Time (s) Ela Time
-------------------------- ------------- ----------- --------
CPU time                         4,851       4,042    55.76
db file sequential read          1,968       1,997    27.55
log file sync                  299,097         369     5.08
db file scattered read          53,031         330     4.55
log file parallel write        302,680         190     2.62
```

In this example, we see that CPU time is the primary source of database delay and improving the speed of the I/O with SSD may not have an appreciable effect on overall Oracle performance.

We also should be aware that it is foolish to focus solely on minimizing physical disk I/O. For databases with sub-optimal SQL statements, we commonly see poor performance combined with a very high data buffer cache hit ratio and very little disk I/O. For these databases, the root cause of the performance problem is excessive logical I/O, whereby the sub-optimal SQL re-reads data blocks over-and-over from the RAM data buffers.

There are several "myths" of Oracle physical I/O that must be exposed at this point:

- All Oracle databases are I/O-bound – Untrue. Databases with a reasonable data buffer cache size and a small working set will usually be constrained by CPU or network latency.

- The Data Buffer Hit Ratio will tell me caching efficiency – Untrue, except in cases of a super-small cache. The Data

---

Buffer Hit Ratio only measures the propensity a data block will be in the buffer on the second I/O request.

- Only a faster disk can remove I/O bottlenecks – This is a common myth. There are other non-RAM approaches to reducing disk I/O for Oracle databases:

- Adjusting optimizer_mode – Oracle will generate widely-differing SQL execution plans depending on the optimizer mode.

- Re-analyze SQL Optimizer statistics – Using better quality CBO statistics (with *dbms_stats*) and adding column histograms can make a huge difference in disk activity.

- Adjusting Oracle parameters – Re-setting the *optimizer_index_cost_adj* and *optimizer_index_caching* parameters can affect physical reads.

- Improve clustering_factor for index range scans - Manually re-sequence table rows to improve *clustering_factor* (sometimes using single-table clusters) can reduce disk I/O.

- Use Materialized Views – Systems with batch-only updates may greatly benefit from Materialized Views to pre-join tables. Of course, the overhead of "refresh commit" is too great for high-update systems.

Now that we understand the historical issues about how Oracle uses RAM, let's look at the issues of duplicated RAM caching in large Oracle systems.

The Problem of Duplicitous RAM Caches

As hardware evolved though the 1990's, Figure 6.7 shows where independent components of database systems started to employ their own RAM caching tools.

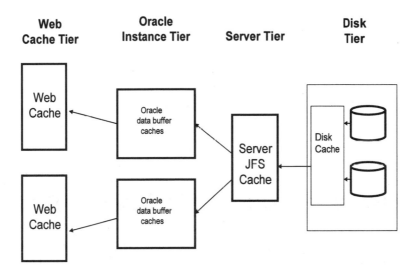

Figure 6.7 – *Multiple RAM caches in an Oracle enterprise*

In this figure, it is clear the Oracle database is not the only component to utilize RAM caching. We see the disk array employs a RAM cache, the servers have a Journal File System (JFS) RAM cache, and the front-end web server also serves to cache Oracle data.

This concept is important because many enterprises may inadvertently double-cache Oracle data. Even more problematic is the "fake" statistics reported by Oracle when multiple-level caches are employed:

- Fake Physical I/O times – If you are using a disk array with a built-in RAM cache, the disk I/O subsystem may "acknowledge" a physical write to Oracle, when in-reality the data has not yet been written to the physical disk spindle. This can skew timing of disk read/write speed.

- Wasted Oracle Data Buffer RAM – In systems that employ web servers, the Apache front-end may cache frequently-used data. Hence, we may waste significant Oracle resources caching data blocks that are already cached on the web server tier.

Now let's move on and look at the best way to use SSD in an Oracle environment. We need to start by examining the relationship between physical disk I/O (POI) and Oracle Logical I/O (LIO).

Why is Oracle Logical I/O So Slow?

As we know, disk latency is generally measured in milliseconds while RAM access is expressed in nanoseconds. In theory, RAM is four orders of magnitude (10,000 times) faster than disk.

However, this is not true when using Oracle. In practice, logical I/O is seldom more than 1,000 times faster than disk I/O. Most Oracle experts say physical disk I/O is only 15 times to 100 times faster than a physical disk I/O.

Oracle has internal data protection mechanisms at work that cause a RAM data block access (a consistent get) to be far slower due to internal locks and latch Serialization mechanisms. This overhead is required by Oracle to maintain read consistency and data concurrency.

So, if Oracle logical I/O is expensive, can this expense be avoided when we read directly from disk? The answer here relates to our discussion about the most appropriate placement for SSD in an Oracle environment.

We also need to note the issue of super-large disks. With 144 gigabyte disks becoming commonplace, I/O intensive database will often see disk latency because many tasks are competing to read blocks on different parts of the super-large disk.

An Oracle physical read must read the disk data block and then transfer it into the Oracle RAM buffer before the data is passed to the requesting program (See Figure 6.8).

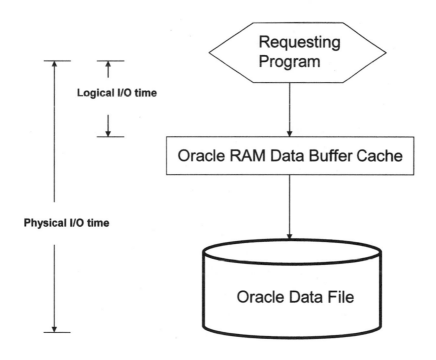

Figure 6.8– *Physical reads include logical I/O latency*

Therefore, if we accept that LIO expense is going to happen regardless of whether or not we perform a PIO, then we can arrive at a valuable insight into the proper placement for SSD in an Oracle environment:

Finding the Baselines

It is critical to remember that Oracle databases are always changing, and the database that you examine at 10:00 AM may be completely different from the database you see at 3:00 PM. Does this mean that a broad-brush application of SSD is not valid?

As shown in Figure 6.9 when we examine the performance of Oracle disk I/O over specific time periods, we see regular "signatures" appear when the I/O information is aggregated by hour-of-the-day and day-of-the-week.

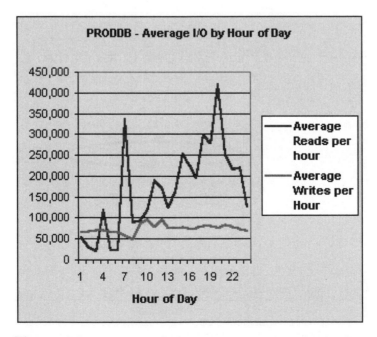

Figure 6.9 – *Average disk reads and writes by hour of the day*

Most Oracle professionals will use Oracle9i STATSPACK or Oracle10g AWR information to gather these baselines. Once we have identified the repeating I/O trends, we will be able to apply a broad-brush to the use of SSD, placing the fast I/O devices where they will do the most good.

We can also capture I/O information at the file level and this gives insights into the best data files to place on super-fast SSD. Here we see the *reads.sql* script that extracts the physical read information from the Oracle 10g *dba_hist_filestatxs* view:

🖫 **reads.sql**

```
-- ***************************************************
-- Copyright © 2003 by Rampant TechPress
-- This script is free for non-commercial purposes
-- with no warranties.  Use at your own risk.
--
-- To license this script for a commercial purpose,
-- contact info@rampant.cc
-- ***************************************************
break on begin_interval_time skip 2

column phyrds   format 999,999,999
column begin_interval_time format a25

select
   begin_interval_time,
   filename,
   phyrds
from
   dba_hist_filestatxs
  natural join
   dba_hist_snapshot
;
```

Below, we see a running total of physical reads by datafile. Note that the snapshots are collected every half-hour. Starting from this script, we could easily add a *where* clause criteria and create a unique time-series exception report.

```
SQL> @reads

BEGIN_INTERVAL_TIME      FILENAME                                   PHYRDS
-----------------------  ----------------------------------------  --------
24-FEB-04 11.00.32.000 PM E:\ORACLE\ORA92\FSDEV10G\SYSTEM01.DBF     164,700
                          E:\ORACLE\ORA92\FSDEV10G\UNDOTBS01.DBF     26,082
                          E:\ORACLE\ORA92\FSDEV10G\SYSAUX01.DBF     472,008
                          E:\ORACLE\ORA92\FSDEV10G\USERS01.DBF        1,794
                          E:\ORACLE\ORA92\FSDEV10G\T_FS_LSQ.ORA       2,123


24-FEB-04 11.30.18.296 PM E:\ORACLE\ORA92\FSDEV10G\SYSTEM01.DBF     167,809
                          E:\ORACLE\ORA92\FSDEV10G\UNDOTBS01.DBF     26,248
                          E:\ORACLE\ORA92\FSDEV10G\SYSAUX01.DBF     476,616
                          E:\ORACLE\ORA92\FSDEV10G\USERS01.DBF        1,795
                          E:\ORACLE\ORA92\FSDEV10G\T_FS_LSQ.ORA       2,244


25-FEB-04 12.01.06.562 AM E:\ORACLE\ORA92\FSDEV10G\SYSTEM01.DBF     169,940
                          E:\ORACLE\ORA92\FSDEV10G\UNDOTBS01.DBF     26,946
                          E:\ORACLE\ORA92\FSDEV10G\SYSAUX01.DBF     483,550
                          E:\ORACLE\ORA92\FSDEV10G\USERS01.DBF        1,799
                          E:\ORACLE\ORA92\FSDEV10G\T_FS_LSQ.ORA       2,248
```

Of course, a little tweaking to the *reads.sql* script and we could report on physical writes, read time, write time, single block reads, and a host of other neat metrics from the *dba_hist_filestatxs* view.

We are now ready to review the existing research on SSD and see what other Oracle experts say about using SSD with Oracle.

A Review of Existing SSD Research Findings

Different researchers are coming to different conclusions about the applicability of SSD to Oracle systems. There are three research papers on SSD and each arrive at similar conclusions. Complete references are included in the References Section at the end of this chapter. Let's take a quick look at the summary findings from each study.

James Morle

According to Morle, 2002, SSD is great for Oracle redo logs, undo tablespace (rollback segment tablespace in Oracle8i), and the TEMP tablespace. He notes that for rollback segments, SSD is a great help:

"This is where SSD can help out. By deploying a single SSD, all redo logs can be located away from the RAID 1+0 array, whilst providing low latency writes and high bandwidth reads (for archiving)."

Morle also asserts that full-caching of a database on SSD may not improve performance,

"If the whole database were running from SSD, there would be enormous pieces of unnecessary work going on, such as:

- o *Management of the buffer cache*
- o *Context switches into kernel mode to perform I/O*
- o *Conversion of the request into SCSI/Fibre Channel*
- o *Transmission across the SAN*
- o *And all the way back again*

In comparison to disk I/O, this whole process is stunningly fast. In comparison to just reading the data straight from user space memory, however, it is incredibly slow!"

Morle notes that a typical OLTP system has a "working set" of frequently referenced data blocks, and those might be good candidates for SSD. For DSS and Data Warehouse systems, Morle advocates moving the "current" table partitions onto SSD devices, leaving the others on traditional disk.

Paul Dorsey

In another landmark SSD study in 2004, Dr, Paul Dorsey showed the data transfer rates for SSD's are always better than traditional disks:

Device	Test#1: Buffered Read	Test #2: Sequential Read	Test #3: Random Read	Test #4: Buffered Write	Test #5: Sequential Write	Test #6: Random Write
RamSan	95	98	98	86	84	82
IDE	85	40	6	65	38	11
SCSI	65	33	9	49	33	11

Dr. Dorsey concludes:

> *"Technologically, SSD is one of the best sources of performance improvement for an Oracle database if you have a typical OLTP system including many transactions which access different small amounts of random data and lots of users.*

> *SSDs may also improve data warehouse applications because of the improved query performance. There is no generic answer for all questions, but solid-state disks represent another way of thinking about managing enterprise-wide databases."*

Woody Hutsell

The Texas Memory Systems whitepaper, titled *Faster Oracle Database Access with the RAMSAN-210* (Hutsell, 2001), Woody Hutsell concludes that certain types of Oracle databases will always benefit from SSD:

> *"There are some databases that should have all of their files moved to solid-state disk. These databases tend to have at least one of the following characteristics:*

> *High concurrent access. Databases that are being hit by a large number of concurrent users should consider storing all of their data on solid-state disk. This will make sure that storage is not a bottleneck for the application and maximize the*

utilization of servers and networks. I/O wait time will be minimized and servers and bandwidth will be fully utilized.

Frequent random accesses to all tables. For some databases, it is impossible to identify a subset of files that are frequently accessed. Many times these databases are effectively large indices.

Small to medium size databases. Given the fixed costs associated with buying RAID systems, it is often economical to buy a solid-state disk to store small to medium sized databases. A RamSan-210, for example, can provide 32GB of database storage for the price of some enterprise RAID systems."

Conclusion

All of the research indicates that SSD can be very valuable to Oracle databases, with the total benefit depending on the type of processing characteristics.

- Use SSD for high-impact files – Experts agree that Oracle redo log files, undo segment and temporary tablespace file will greatly benefit from SSD.

- SSD has impressive speed improvements - (Dorsey, 2004) reported a 67% gain (.67x) in data access speed with SSD. (Morle, 2002) noted a reported a 25% (.25x) increase in system speed with SSD

- SSD may shift the Oracle bottleneck to CPU – SSD should only be attempted when CPU consumption (as measured by a STATSPACK top-5 wait event report) is less than 50% of the consumption. Using SSD will shift the bottleneck from I/O to CPU, and the server may require more CPU's to improve dispatching, or faster CPU's (e.g. Itanium2 processors).

- Read-intensive system benefit most from SSD – Write-intensive systems, especially those with high buffer invalidations, may only see a marginal speed improvement.

- SSD will speed-up access on super-large disks – The 114 gigabyte disk often experience disk enqueue as competing tasks wait their turn at the read-write heads. SSD will surely improve throughput for these types of database disks.

References:

Dorsey, P, Solid State Disks: *"Sorting out the Myths from the Reality"*, *IOUG SELECT Magazine* (2004)

Morle, J, *Solid State Disks in an Oracle Environment: The New Rules of Deployment*, Scale Abilities Ltd., 2002.

Hutsell, W, *Faster Oracle Database Access with the RAMSAN-210*, Texas Memory Systems, http://www.storagesearch.com/texasmemsysart1.pdf

Oracle 10g Disk Related Features

Automatic Storage Management

In Oracle Database 10g, Oracle has expanded upon the Oracle Disk Management and Oracle Managed Files that where available in 9i. In 10g, Oracle provides Automatic Storage Management (ASM), a total disk management interface for Oracle files.

Automatic Storage Management is a database service that allows efficient management of disk drives providing nearly 24/7 availability. It assists the DBA with managing potentially thousands of database files across multiple database instances. It does so by creating disk groups, which are comprised of disks and the files that reside on them. With it, the DBA only needs to manage a smaller number of disk groups.

ASM Concepts

When using ASM, the DBA creates a database structure such as a tablespaces, archive logs, redo logs, or control files, he/she needs to specify the file location for the structure in terms of disk groups. Then the Automatic Storage Mechanism (ASM) will create and manage the underlying files for the structures within the ASM managed disk groups.

Adding ASM will not eliminate any existing database functionality. ASM is used in conjunction with the existing database functionalities with file systems or raw devices, and

Oracle Managed Files (OMF) as in previous versions. In an environment with different database versions, older versions or existing databases can use storage with file systems or with storage on raw devices, as they have always done in the past. New files can be created as ASM files, while old files are administered the traditional way. In a nutshell, we can have a mixture of ASM files; Oracle managed files, and manually managed files all at the same time. Existing files can be migrated to ASM if needed.

ASM is responsible for file management and prevents accidental file deletion by eliminating the file system interface. It provides raw disk I/O performance for all files, striping them across multiple storage arrays. It reduces the cost of managing storage with a clustered volume manager and integrated file system functionality.

ASM adds the reliability features found in LVM (Logical Volume Managers) such as mirroring protection, eliminating the purchase of third party products. Similarly, in a RAC environment, ASM eliminates the need for a Cluster LVM or Cluster File System (CFS). However, the Oracle cluster ready services are still required in 10g.

ASM also offers the benefits of mirroring and striping. An advantage of ASM over conventional VMS is the file based storage policy is generally more reliable than the volume based. Hence, the same disk group can have a combination of files protected by mirroring or no protection.

ASM Architecture

For the ASM architecture, Oracle Database 10g utilizes a separate small Oracle instance (it has no database associated with it, it is only the instance), created during database set up.

An ASM instance manages the metadata that is needed to make ASM files available to the "regular" database instances. The ASM instance and database instances have to have access to a common set of disks called disk groups. The normal Database instances communicate with an ASM instance only to get information about the layout of these files and to access the contents of ASM files directly. To create a database that uses storage managed by ASM, we have to first start with the ASM instance.

An ASM instance has two new background process types - one for coordinating the disk group rebalance activity and one for data extent movements (ORB0, ORB1, etc.). Also, each database instance using ASM has two new background processes called OSMB and RBAL. In a database instance, OSMB connects to foreground processes in ASM instances. RBAL performs global calls to open the disks in disk groups. Using these connections, periodic messages are exchanged to update statistics and to verify that both instances are running healthy. For certain database operations like file creation, ASM intervention is required and the database foreground connects directly to the ASM instance. Whenever a connection is made to the ASM instance and OSMB process is started dynamically.

The basic component of Automatic Storage Management is the disk group. We configure ASM by creating disk groups, which in database instances, can be used as the default location for files created in the database. Oracle provides SQL statements for us to create and manage disk groups, their contents and their metadata. The disk groups are built on raw filesystems.

Group services are used to register the connection information needed by the database instances to find ASM instances. Group Services are a part of Oracle's portable clusterware, which gets automatically installed on every node that runs Oracle10g. Due to its automatic striping and load balancing capabilities, ASM all but eliminates the need for manual disk tuning.

The ASM hierarchy can be explained using a diagram. Compare it with previous versions of Oracle database.

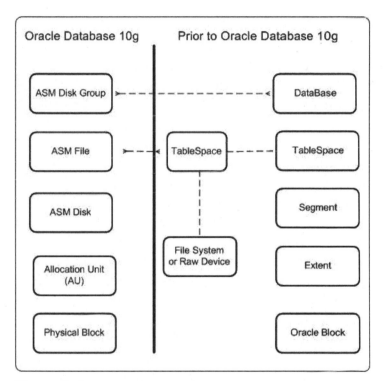

Figure 7.1 *Automatic Storage Management Hierarchy*

A datafile from a tablespace can be stored as an *ASM file*, as a *file system file* or a *raw device*. Each ASM file belongs to a single *disk group*. A disk group may contain files belonging to several databases, and a single database may form multiple disk groups. ASM files are always spread across all the disks in the disk group. Normal files are spread in 1 megabyte stripes while serial access files such as redo logs are spread in 128k stripes. ASM files can be created for redo log files, temporary files, RMAN files, parameter files and Data Pump dump files.

ASM introduces the concept of an *allocation unit* (AU), the smallest contiguous disk space allocated by the ASM. The typical value for an AU is 1MB and is not user configurable. ASM does not allow physical blocks to be split across allocation units.

A disk group is a collection of disks managed as a *logical unit*. With in a disk group, I/Os are balanced across all the disks. Each disk group has its own file directory, disk directory, and other directories.

For better database performance, dissimilar disks should be partitioned into separate disk groups. The redundancy characteristics are set up while defining a disk group. EXTERNAL REDUNDANCY indicates that ASM does not provide any redundancy for the disk group. NORMAL REDUNDANCY (default) prompts the disk group to tolerate the loss of a single failure without data loss. HIGH REDUNDANCY provides a greater degree of protection (three way mirroring). ASM provides near-optimal I/O balancing with out any manual tuning.

A *failure group* is a set of disks with in a particular disk group that share a common resource whose failure needs to be tolerated. For example, a failure of the SCSI controller leads to all its associated disks becoming unavailable, though each of the disks is functional. Failure groups are used to identify which disks are used to store redundant data. If two-way mirroring is specified for a file (say the redo), then redundant copies of file extents must be stored in separate failure groups.

Storage is added or removed form disk groups in units of *ASM disks*. ASM files are Oracle database files stored in ASM disk groups. When a file is created, certain file attributes like protection policy (mirroring or none), striping policy are set. These files are visible to RMAN and other Oracle supplied tools, but are invisible from the operating system and its utilities.

Templates are provided to simplify file creation by mapping complex file attribute specifications about ASM files (in ASM disk groups) to a single name. For example, a template named ARCHIVELOG provides the file redundancy and striping attributes for all archive log files written to ASM disks. A list of templates is given later in this chapter.

With ASM file, operations are specified in terms of *database objects*. The names of the file are exposed through some data dictionary view or the ALTER DATABASE BACKUP CONTROLFILE TO TRACE command. The DBA never requires knowing filenames for database administration.

The use of ASM filename formats depends on the context of file usage like referencing an existing file, creating a single file or creating multiple files.

Fully qualified filenames specify a disk group name, a database name, a file type, a type-specific tag, a file number and an incarnation number. The fully qualified name is generated for every ASM file on its creation. We will learn more about fully qualified names later in this chapter.

Numeric names are derived from the fully qualified name. You, the DBA can specify user-friendly alias names for ASM files. Alias names are used for existing as well as new ASM files. But, you must create a hierarchical directory structure for these alias names. Incomplete filenames with disk group names are used only for ASM file creation operations

ASM Instance Management

Automatic Storage Management is installed by default with Oracle Universal Installer. The Database Configuration Assistance (DBCA) looks for an existing ASM instance and if it does not find one, you have the option if creating and configuring one during the installation process.

An ASM instance is started like any other database instance, except that the initialization parameter file contains the parameter *instance_type=OSM*. For ASM instances, the mount option doesn't try to mount a database, but tries to mount the disk groups that are specified by the *osm_diskgroups* initialization parameter. ASM instances require a much smaller SGA (typically 64 MB) and should be brought up automatically on sever reboots and must be running at all times for other databases to be able to run. In a startup, the ASM instance must be started before any of its dependent database, in a shutdown it must be shutdown last. If you use *dbstart* and *dbshut* scripts for automatic startup and shutdown, have the ASM instance first in the *oratab* file used by *dbstart*, create a second *oratab* file that places the ASM instance last for shutdown and point the *dbshut* script at it. The ASM instance can be shutdown like any other database instance using similar commands.

The DBA can use the Oracle Enterprise Manager (OEM) or the Database Configuration Assistant (DBCA) for a GUI interface to connect to ASM to configure and alter disk groups and their metadata. OEM provides an integrated approach for managing the ASM instance as well as database instances, while DBCA is for database instances only.

An ASM instance does not have a data dictionary. So, you can only connect to an ASM instance as SYSDBA or SYSOPER. For connecting remotely to an ASM instance, you have to use the password file. No other user administration is maintained by ASM instance. Those who connect to the ASM instance with SYSDBA privilege have complete administrative access to all disk groups in the system.

The SYSOPER privilege is limited to the following SQL commands only.

```
STARTUP AND SHUTDOWN,
ALTER DISKGROUP MOUNT/DISMOUNT/REPAIR
ALTER DISKGROUP ONLINE/OFFLINE DISK
ALTER DISKGROUP REBALANCE/CHECK
```

Access to all *v$asm_* * views (discussed later in this chapter).

Initialization Parameters for ASM Instance

While there are a lot of initialization parameters meant for the database instance, only a handful is relevant for the ASM instance. Here is a list of ASM initialization parameters.

- *instance_type* - Must be set to *ASM*. <u>This is the only required parameter</u>. All other parameters assume defaults suited for most environments.

- *db_unique_name* - Unique name for ASM (or group of instances) with in the cluster or on node. Default is +ASM.

- *asm_diskstring* - Limits the set of disks that ASM considers for recovery. Default is NULL.

- *asm_diskgroups* - List of names of disk groups mounted by ASM instance at startup or when ALTER DISKGROUP

ALL MOUNT is used. Default is NULL. If you are using SPFILE, you may rarely need to alter this dynamic value.

- *asm_power_limit* - The maximum power on an ASM instance for disk rebalancing. Default is 1.

Parameters that start with ASM can be set only for ASM instances. If you specify a database initialization parameter in an ASM init parameter file, it will cause one of the following scenarios. For an invalid parameter, the ASM instance will produce an ORA-15021 error. For parameters related to buffer cache and dump destinations valid for ASM instance, the values will be accepted. If on the other hand, we specify an ASM specific parameter in a database instance, it will produce an ORA-15021 error.

Disk Recovery Time

The *asm_diskstring* initialization parameter is used to limit the set of disks considered for recovery, and is dependent on the operating system for its allowed format (a valid path to the RAW device files). When a new disk is added to the disk group, every ASM instance that has this disk group mounted will be able to see the new disk using its *asm_diskstring* parameter. The default value of NULL is sufficient for most cases. NULL will cause ASM to find all disks in platform specific locations with read/write access. With a more restrictive value, the ASM can reduce the time required for discovery and thus improve time to add disk to the disk group or disk group mount time.

Rebalance Operation

The Oracle database can perform one rebalance operation per rebalance processes on disks at a given time on an ASM instance. The number of rebalance processes is set by the value of *asm_power_limit*. This parameter can be changed dynamically. With a higher value, a faster rebalance operation will take place and vice versa for a lower value.

The *v$aasm_operation* view provides information that can be used for adjusting the power of *asm_power_limit* and the rebalance operations. If the DESIRED_POWER_COLUMN is less than the ACTUAL_POWER_COLUMN for a rebalance operation, then the *asm_power_limit* will impact it. This view also gives an estimate of the amount of time remaining to complete the operation through the EST_MINUTES column

The *asm_power_limit* value has an impact on the resource consumption of the server. A lower value of *asm_power_limit* frees up CPU and I/O bandwidth used for rebalance operation by the ASM. This will leave the resources available for other applications. The default value is meant to minimize any disruptions to other applications.

ASM Instance Operations

As we have seen in earlier sections of this chapter, an ASM instance is similar to any other oracle instance except that its initialization parameter file contains *instance_type = ASM,* and it is not associated with an actual Oracle database. This parameter differentiates it as an ASM instance to the Oracle executable. Oracle recommends the use of a server parameter file (*spfile*) as a *spfile* will eliminate any chances of errors with manual editing. Also, when you use an ASM instance, make sure that it is created with sufficient SGA as in a small database instance. Around 32MB to 64MB SGA is sufficient for small to medium sized ASM instance installations.

Starting Up and Shutting Down of an ASM Instance

The STARTUP command in SQL*Plus tries to mount the disk groups specified in *asm_diskgroups* instead of the database. ASM interprets other extensions to STARTUP command as given below.

- MOUNT - mounts the disk groups specified by *asm_diskgroups* or already configured in the ASM instance.

- NOMOUNT - doesn't mount any disk groups, but starts up the ASM instance.

- OPEN - not valid for an ASM instance.

- FORCE - issues the command SHUTDOWN ABORT to the ASM instance and restarts it.

Shutting down and ASM instance is like any other database instance. Just issue the command SHUTDOWN NORMAL and the instance goes down. You can also add extensions to the SHUTDOWN command as given below.

- NORMAL - ASM waits for the connected ASM instances and other active ASM SQL sessions to exit before shutting down.

- IMMEDIATE - ASM waits for SQL sessions in progress to finish before shutting down. Database instances need not be   disconnected to shutdown the instance.

- ABORT - ASM immediately shuts down.

- TRANSACTIONAL - Similar to IMMEDIATE.

Discovering the Disks and Disk Groups

We have seen that an ASM instance reads the *asm_diskstring* initialization parameter during startup, if it is specified, which has information on all disks in the disk groups.   This parameter saves you from adding paths for all disks in disk groups to the initialization parameter file. To mount a disk group, ASM has to find all the disks in that particular group. So, all disk configuration errors have to be resolved, before mounting a disk group. This feature also helps in recovery of ASM instances.

An ASM instance updates ASM metadata and writes to the disk group log during its operation. After it fails and *on* reinitializes, it reads the disk group log and recovers all transient changes.

ASM Instance Configuration

If you need to manage the ASM components, there are certain rules and steps to be considered throughout the process. Let's go over the limits and rules governing ASM.

Automatic Storage Management has the following operational limits:

- A maximum of 63 disk groups for every storage system

- A maximum of 10,000 ASM disks for every storage system

- A maximum storage of 4 petabytes for each ASM disk

- A maximum storage of 40 exabytes for each storage system.

- A maximum of 1 million files for each disk group

- A maximum of 2.4 terabyte storage for each file.

To get an idea of the storage in terms of kilobytes, use the following table.

Prefix	Symbol	X bytes
mega	M	1000 kilobytes
giga	G	1000 megabytes
tera	T	1000 gigabytes
peta	P	1000 terabytes
exa	E	10,00,000 terabytes

Table 7.1 *Storage Limits*

Rules and Guidelines for ASM Instance Configuration

When you use more than one disk in a disk group, they should have similar size and performance characteristics. It is better to group disks according to their size and performance. Keep disks with dissimilar characteristics for maintenance purposes only, if absolutely needed. Also, keep separate disk groups for database files, control files, and flash recovery areas.

If you are using storage array disks, don't divide the physical volumes into logical volumes, as it will interfere with ASM operation. To the ASM instance, any such disk division will hide the physical disk boundaries and hinder its performance.

ASM requires a minimum of 2 failure groups for normal redundancy disk groups, while 3 failure groups are needed for high redundancy groups. If a lesser number is provided in either case, reliability of the system is affected.

ASM allows dynamically adding and removing disks in a disk group with out data loss. ASM will reallocate files in such a manner that rebalancing of data will not cause database instance to shutdown. A disk cannot be removed from a disk group until the data on it is offloaded to another disk.

Similarly, a new disk cannot support any I/O operations, until the disk group data is re-balanced to take advantage of it. Adding and removing disks will temporarily cause a performance impact on I/O operations. So be judicious in scheduling these operations so as not to impact a production environment.

Creating a Disk Group

First, create a set of raw volumes across several disks that in total, equals the size of the desired disk group.

Then, a disk group is created using the CREATE DISK GROUP command. You can specify the raw disk partitions that are to be formatted as ASM disks under the disk group. You can also specify the failure groups, and redundancy level for each disk group. The redundancy level can be NORMAL REDUNDANCY, HIGH REDUNDANCY, or EXTERNAL REDUNDANCY. The NORMAL and HIGH options are defined by disk group templates, while EXTERNAL is for external disk groups like storage arrays.

ASM calculates the size of each disk. To limit the size of a disk, use the SIZE clause for each disk. You can name the disks on your own or ASM will create operating system independent names for the disks as default.

The ASM instance verifies that a disk in a disk group is addressable and usable. It reads the first block of the disk to determine if it belongs to a group and writes a header to disks not in any group.

A disk can belong to only one disk group. You can force a disk in a disk group to become a member of another disk group by using the FORCE clause in the command. For this, the original disk group should not be mounted and the disk must have a disk group header. NOFORCE is the default and it will read only disks that are not part of other disk groups.

When you issue the CREATE DISKGROUP command, it mounts the disk group for the first time and adds the disk group name to the *asm_diskgroups* initialization parameter in *spfile*. If you are using *init.ora* file and need the disk group to be automatically mounted at startup, you have to manually add the disk group name to the *asm_diskgroups* entry.

Let's look at an example, which will be used through out the rest of this chapter. The *asm_diskstring* is set to '/dev/*'. The following are the disks in /dev - /dska01, /dska02, /dskb01, /dskb02. /dska01 and /dska02 are on a separate SCSI controller from other disks.

```
CREATE DISKGROUP dskgrp01 NORMAL REDUNDANCY.

FAILGROUP fgcontrol01 DISK '/dev/dska01', '/dev/dska02',

FAILGROUP fgcontrol02 DISK '/dev/dskb01', '/dev/dskb02' ;
```

Here the *dskgrp01* is made up of 4 disks belonging to failure groups: *fgcontrol01* or *fgcontrol02*. With the NORMAL REDUNDANCY option, ASM provides redundancy for all files in *dskgrp01* and *dskgrp02* subject to the attributes given in the disk group templates.

Since we did not specify any names to the disks using NAME clause, they will be named as *dskgrp01_0001, dskgrp01_0002, dskgrp01_0003,* and *dskgrp01_0004.*

Altering a Disk Group (add, drop, undrop, resize, rebalance)

After creating a disk group, you use the ALTER DISKGROUP command to add, drop or resize any disk(s).

This command can be used for multiple disks in one statement. After you issue an ALTER DISKGROUP statement, ASM rebalances the file extents automatically to suit the new disk group configuration. The rebalancing operation continues as a long running operation, even after the ALTER DISKGROUP command completes successfully. The progress of this rebalancing task can be viewed from *v$asm_operation*.

To add a disk '/dska03' to the 'dskgrp01' disk group, use the ADD DISK clause as in the following command:

```
ALTER DISKGROUP dskgrp01 ADD DISK '/dev/dska03' ;
```

This command adds the disk and assigns 'dska03' to its own FAILGROUP as none was specified in the command.

If you want to add a handful of disks (/dskc01, /dskc02, /dskc03) under a different failure group (fgcontrol03), issue the following command:

```
ALTER DISKGROUP dskgrp01 NORMAL REDUNDANCY
FAILGROUP fgcontrol03 DISK '/dev/dskc*' ;
```

To drop a disk from a disk group, use the DROP DISK clause of ALTER DISKGROUP command. For dropping all the disks in a failure group, use the DROP DISKS IN FAILUREGROUP clause of ALTER DSIKGROUP command. When a disk is dropped, the files in the dropped disk are moved to other disks in the disk groups and the header entry on dropped disk is cleared. With the FORCE clause of DROP operation, the disk is dropped with out waiting for ASM to read or write to the disk. FORCE clause is possible only for disk groups made under NORMAL or HIGH REDUNDANCY options.

To drop the disk '/dska03' from the 'dskgrp01' disk group, use the DROP DISK clause as in the following command.

```
ALTER DISKGROUP dskgrp01 DROP DISK '/dev/dska03' ;
```

You can drop a disk and add another one at the same time in a single command as follows.

```
ALTER DISKGROUP dskgrp01 DROP DISK '/dev/dska03'

ADD FAILGROUP fgcontrol04 DISK '/dev/dskd01', '/dev/dskd02' ;
```

To cancel a drop operation of all disks in a diskgroup, we can use the UNDROP DISKS clause of ALTER DISKGROUP command. This statement will cancel all pending drop disk operations with in a disk group. If the statement has completely finished, this statement will not work. Also UNDROP DISKS will restore disks that are being dropped as part of DROP DISKGROUP or FORCE statements.

```
ALTER DISKGROUP dskgrp01 UNDROP DISKS;
```

To resize a disk or all disks in a disk group or a failure group, use the RESIZE clause of ALTER DISKGROUP command. The RESIZE option needs a *size* parameter, otherwise it will resize the disks to the size of the disk as returned by the operating system. The new size after the RESIZE operation is written to the ASM disk header record. If the new size is higher, it is immediately available for utilization, while a lower size will require the completion of rebalance operation.

After you issue the RESIZE command to reduce the size of a disk, the rebalance operation tries to reallocate the files among other disks. The RESIZE command will fail if the extents cannot be successfully transferred and rebalanced. Similarly, the RESIZE command fails if you resize a disk to values higher than disk capacity.

Assume that the disks in above examples were of 168 GB size. To reduce the size of /dska01 to 120 GB, use the following command.

```
ALTER DISKGROUP dskgrp01
RESIZE DISK '/dev/dska01' SIZE 120G;
```

To reduce the size of all disks under failgroup fgcontrol01, modify the command as follows.

```
ALTER DISKGROUP dskgrp01
RESIZE DISKS IN FAILGROUP fgcontrol01 SIZE 120G;
```

Manual rebalancing of a disk group is possible with the REBALANCE clause of the ALTER DISKGROUP command. A manual rebalance is seldom needed, but if the DBA feels that speed of rebalance operation is not enough, this command is deployed.

Remember that we learned about *adm_power_limit* in ASM architecture. This parameter has a profound effect on the rebalance operation as follows. The POWER clause used along with REBALANCE option specifies the degree of parallelism and speed of the rebalance operation. The POWER value can be set from 0 to 11 (1 is default), where 0 stops rebalancing and 11 is the fastest. The speed of an ongoing operation can be changed by altering the POWER with a new level. With a zero value for POWER, the rebalance is stopped until the value is reset.

THE *asm_power_limit* controls the degree of parallelization for rebalance operations. Even with a value of POWER at eleven (11), the degree of parallelization will not exceed the value specified in *asm_power_limit* (default = 1). Therefore, the rebalance operation is limited by the above initialization parameter.

An example for a rebalance operation with *asm_power_limit* of 10 is as follows.

```
ALTER DISKGROUP dskgroup01 REBALANCE POWER 10;
```

Mounting Disk Groups

We have seen that disk groups located in the path specified in the *asm_diskgroups* initialization parameter are automatically mounted at the ASM instance startup. These are also un-mounted when ASM instance is shutdown. ASM will mount a new disk group when you initially create it and un-mount it when you drop it.

The ALTER DISKGROUP.. MOUNT (UNMOUNT) command is used whenever you want to do manual operations on a disk group. These operations can be performed, by calling the disk groups by name or using ALL. To dismount a disk group with open files, use the FORCE clause of the DISMOUNT option.

To dismount an individual disk group, use the following command:

```
ALTER DISKGROUP dskgrp01 dismount;
```

To mount dskgrp01 back to normal, issue the command.

```
ALTER DISKGROUP dskgrp01 mount;
```

For dismounting all disk groups in our above examples, use the ALL clause as follows:

```
ALTER DISKGROUP ALL DISMOUNT;
```

Disk Group Templates

What exactly is a disk group template? A disk group template is a collection of attributes that are applied to all files created with in the disk group. We get a set of initial default templates from Oracle for use by ASM. The *v$asm_template* view gives a list of all templates identifiable by the ASM instance. We can add new templates to a disk group, modify existing ones and even drop them using ALTER DISKGROUP statement.

Here is a table listing all commonly used ASM system default templates.

NAME OF TEMPLATE	TYPE OF TILE	NORMAL REDUN-DANCY	HIGH	EXTERNAL REDUN-DANCY	STRIP-ING
ARCHIVELOG	Archive logs	2-Way Mirroring	3-Way Mirroring	Unprotected	Coarse
AUTOBACKUP	Automatic backup files	2-Way Mirroring	3-Way Mirroring	Unprotected	Coarse
BACKUPSET	Datafile, datafile incremental, archive log - backups	2-Way Mirroring	3-Way Mirroring	Unprotected	Coarse
CONTROL	Control files	2-Way Mirroring	3-Way Mirroring	Unprotected	Fine
DATAFILE	Datafiles	2-Way Mirroring	3-Way Mirroring	Unprotected	Coarse
DATAGUARDCONFIG	Disaster recovery configuration	2-Way Mirroring	3-Way Mirroring	Unprotected	Coarse
DUMPSET	Data Pump dump	2-Way Mirroring	3-Way Mirroring	Unprotected	Coarse
FLASHBACK	Flashback log	2-Way Mirroring	3-Way Mirroring	Unprotected	Fine

NAME OF TEMPLATE	TYPE OF TILE	NORMAL REDUN-DANCY	HIGH	EXTERNAL REDUN-DANCY	STRIP-ING
ONLINELOG	Online log	2-Way Mirroring	3-Way Mirroring	Unprotected	Fine
PARAMETERFILE	SPFILE	2-Way Mirroring	3-Way Mirroring	Unprotected	Coarse
TEMPFILE	Tempfile	2-Way Mirroring	3-Way Mirroring	Unprotected	Coarse

Table 7.2 *ASM Default Templates*

To add a template for a disk group, use the ADD TEMPLATE clause of the ALTER DISKGROUP command along with its attributes. Let us assume that the DBA wants to create several templates for use in different projects and that DBAHELPER1 is the required template for dskgrp01.

```
ALTER DISKGROUP dskgrp01 ADD TEMPLATE DBAHELPER1 ATTRIBUTES (MIRROR
FINE);
```

The above statement will create a template with the following attributes to files.

NAME OF TEMPLATE	NORMAL REDUNDANCY	HIGH REDUNDANCY	EXTERNAL REDUNDANCY	STRIPING
DBAHELPER1	2-Way Mirroring	3-Way Mirroring	Cannot be specified	64 KB

To modify an existing template, use the ALTER TEMPLATE clause. When you use the ALTER TEMPLATE command on an existing template (system defined or user defined), only specified attributes are changed. Unspecified attribute specifications are left untouched. Also, when an existing template is modified, new files created using that template are affected. Existing files continue to retain their attributes.

Oracle Disk I/O Tuning

To change the striping for the DBAHELPER1 template, use the following command:

```
ALTER DISKGROUP dskgrp01 ALTER TEMPLATE DBAHELPER1 ATTRIBUTES
(COARSE);
```

To drop an existing template, use the DROP TEMPLATE clause. This can be applied to one or more templates from a disk group. System defined templates supplied by Oracle cannot be dropped. Only user-defined templates can be dropped.

To drop the DBAHELPER1 template, issue the following command:

```
ALTER DISKGROUP dskgrp01 DROP TEMPLATE DBAHELPER1;
Disk Group Directories
```

A disk group contains a hierarchical directory structure with fully qualified file names (system alias) along with alias filenames. On a new file creation, the system alias is automatically created by ASM. To create more friendly aliases for filenames, you have to create a directory structure to support the new naming conventions.

To create a new directory, use the ADD DIRECTORY clause of ALTER DISKGROUP command. The directory path should begin with a plus (+) sign, followed by subdirectory names separated by forward slash (/) characters.

An example using the *dskgrp01* disk group would be as follows:

```
ALTER DISKGROUP dskgrp01 ADD DIRECTORY '+dskgrp01/new10gdb';
```

To add a new directory called 'newuser' under 'new10gdb', use the following command. Care should be taken to see that relative paths are accurate and that no subdirectory is left out in this process.

```
ALTER DISKGROUP dskgrp01 ADD DIRECTORY '+dskgrp01/new10gdb/newuser';
```

To rename a directory, use the RENAME DIRECTOY clause as follows:

```
ALTER DISKGROUP dskgrp01 RENAME DIRECTORY
'+dskgrp01/new10gdb/newuser' to '+dskgrp01/new10gdb/createuser';
```

Similar to diskgroup templates, we can drop a directory. To drop a directory, use the DROP DIRECTORY clause. System created directories cannot be dropped. Use the FORCE clause to drop directory with contents.

In our above example, new10gdb directory has *createuser* underneath it in the tree structure. To drop the new 10gdb directory, use the following command:

```
ALTER DISKGROUP dskgrp01 DROP DIRECTORY '+dskgrp01/new10gdb' FORCE;
```

Alias Filenames

Once you have the directory structure in place, you can add alias names to provide more meaningful names to ASM files. Use the ADD ALIAS, RENAME ALIAS, or DELETE ALIAS clauses of the ALTER DISKGROUP command to add, rename or delete alias names, except for system alias. The *v$asm_alias* view has information on every alias known to the ASM instance. If the alias is system generated, it will be specified under SYSTEM_CREATED column.

COLUMN	DATA TYPE	DESCRIPTION
NAME	VARCHAR2(48)	ASM Alias or alias directory name

GROUP_NUMBER	NUMBER	Owning disk group number of the alias
FILE_NUMBER	NUMBER	ASM file number of the alias
FILE_INCARNATION	NUMBER	ASM file incarnation number for the alias
ALIAS_INDEX	NUMBER	Alias entry number for the alias
ALIAS_INCARNATION	NUMBER	Incarnation number for the parent of the alias
PARENT_INDEX	NUMBER	Number of the directory containing the alias
REFERENCE_INDEX	NUMBER	Number of the directory describing the current entry. REFERENCE_INDEX = 0, for alias entries.
ALIAS_DIRECTORY	VARCHAR2(1)	Alias is to a directory (Y) or to ASM (N)
SYSTEM_CREATED	VARCHAR2(1)	Alias is system created (Y) or user created (N)

Table 7.3 *ASM Default Templates*

To add an alias name for an ASM filename, use the ADD ALIAS clause with full directory path and the alias.

```
ALTER DISKGROUP dskgrp01 ADD ALIAS
'+dskgrp01/new10gdb/SALES_TBL01.dbf' FOR
'+dgroup1/qadata/testdb1/sales.325.1' ;
```

The same command can be specified with the numeric form of the ASM filename as follows:

```
ALTER DISKGROUP dskgrp01 ADD ALIAS
'+dgroup01/new10gdb/SALES_TBL01.dbf' FOR '+dskgrp1.325.1' ;
```

To rename an alias name, use the RENAME ALIAS clause with full directory path and the alias.

```
ALTER DISKGROUP dskgrp01 RENAME ALIAS
'+dskgrp01/SALESDB/salesdata_1.dbf' FOR
'+dgroup1/qadata/testdb2/sales.325.3' ;
```

To drop an alias name, use the DELETE ALIAS clause with full directory path and the alias. It is very important to note that dropping an alias will not remove the underlying file on the file system.

```
ALTER DLSKGROUP dskgrp01 DELETE ALIAS
'+dskgrp01/SALESDB/salesdata_1.dbf';
```

To drop files and associated alias names from a disk group, use the DROP FILE clause of the ALTER DISKGROUP command. In our above example, we dropped the alias '+dskgrp01/SALESDB/salesdata_1.dbf', but still left the file on the system.

To remove the file along with its alias name, issue the following command:

```
ALTER DISKGROUP dskgrp01 DROP FILE
'+dskgrp01/SALESDB/salesdata_1.dbf';
```

You can also use the system-generated alias in the DROP FILE command.

```
ALTER DISKGROUP dskgrp01 DROP FILE
'+dgroup1/qadata/testdb2/sales.325.3';
```

Dropping a Disk Group

We can drop an ASM disk group with the DROP DISKGROUP command and optionally its files using the INCLUDING CONTENTS clause. The default option for

DROP DISKGROUP is EXCLUDING CONTENTS, which prevents dropping a disk group with contents.

To drop a disk group, the ASM instance has to be up and running, the disk group has to be mounted and no files in the disk group should be open. The DROP DISKGROUP command returns after the action is completed. This command will remove the disk group name from the *asm_diskgroups* parameter when server parameter file is used. With *init.ora* files, the disk group has to be manually removed from the *asm_diskgroups* parameter after the DROP operation and before the next shutdown of the ASM instance.

To drop *dskgrp01* with its contents, use the following command:

```
DROP DISKGROUP dskgrp01 INCLUDING CONTENTS
```

Internal Consistency of Disk Groups

After doing any of the above operations to disk groups, you may want to verify the internal consistency of the disk group metadata. For this purpose, use the ALTER DISKGROUP .... CHECK command. We can check specific files, some disks or all disks in a disk group, or specific failure groups in a disk group. The disc group has to be in mounted state for these checks.

ASM will attempt to correct any errors during this operation. If there are any errors, it will be displayed and also written to alert log. Unless the user specifies a NOREPAIR clause, ASM will fix any error situation.

To check the consistency in the metadata for all disks in the dskgrp01 disk group, use the following command:

```
ALTER DISKGROUP dskgrp01 CHECK ALL;
```

File Types Supported by ASM

ASM supports most file types in a database. But, some administrative file types (audit files, alert log, backup files, export file, and trace file) cannot be supported on an ASM disk group. The following table lists the different file types, ASM support, and system default templates for their file creation.

FILE TYPE	ASM SUPPORTED	DEFAULT TEMPLATES
Archive Log Backup	YES	BACKUPSET
Archive Log	YES	ARCHIVELOG
Change Tacking File	YES	CHANGETRACKING
Control File	YES	CONTROLFILE
Data Pump Dump	YES	DUMPSET
Data File Backup	YES	BACKUPSET
Data File Copy	YES	DATAFILE
Data file	YES	DATAFILE
Disaster Recovery Configurations	YES	DATAGUARDCONFIG
Flashback Log	YES	FLASHBACK
Operating System File	NO	NOT APPLICABLE
SPFILE	YES	PARAMETERFILE
Redo Log	YES	ONLINELOG
Temporary File	YES	TEMPFILE
Trace File	NO	NOT APPLICABLE

Table 7.4 *File types, ASM support, and system default templates*

Dynamic Performance Views on ASM

The following views are useful to get more information on Automatic Storage Management. These views are available in ASM instance as well as database instances. We will go over the views in ASM instances and compare it with a database instance.

v$asm_diskgroup – has information about disk group in an ASM instance. In a database instance, it has one row for every mounted ASM disk group.

COLUMN	DESCRIPTION
GROUP_NUMBER	Cluster-wide number for the disk group
NAME	disk group's name
SECTOR_SIZE	Physical block size in bytes
BLOCK_SIZE	ASM metadata block size in bytes
ALLOCATION_UNIT_SIZE	Allocation unit size in bytes
STATE	State of the disk group relative to the database instance - CONNECTED, BROKEN, UNKNOWN, MOUNTED, DISMOUNTED
TYPE	Redundancy type - NORMAL, HIGH, EXTERN
TOTAL_MB	Total disk group capacity in megabytes
FREE_MB	Unused capacity in megabytes

v$asm_disk - has information about all disks in an ASM instance, which are independent or part of disk groups. In a database instance, it has one row for every mounted disk.

COLUMN	DESCRIPTION
GROUP_NUMBER	Cluster-wide number for the disk group containing the disk (foreign key to v$asm_diskgroup)
DISK_NUMBER	Disk number within its disk group
COMPOUND_INDEX	32-bit number with disk group number and disk number
INCARNATION	Incarnation number for the disk
MOUNT_STATUS	Per-instance status of the disk relative to group mounts - OPENED, CLOSED, MISSING,CACHED
HEADER_STATUS	Status of the disk per instance - MEMBER, FORMER, CANDIDATE, UNKNOWN, INCOMPATIBLE, PROVISIONED,CONFLICT
MODE_STATUS	Global status about kinds of I/O requests allowed to the disk - ONLINE, OFFLINE, UNKNOWN
STATE	Global state of the disk with respect to its disk group - NORMAL, HUNG, ADDING, DROPPING, FORCING, DROPPED, UNKNOWN
REDUNDANCY	External redundancy of the disk - MIRROR, PARITY, UNPROT, UNKNOWN
LIBRARY	Library name that discovered the disk
TOTAL_MB	Total disk capacity in megabytes

COLUMN	DESCRIPTION
FREE_MB	Unused disk capacity in megabytes
NAME	Disk name
FAILGROUP	Failure group name containing the disk
LABEL	Disk label name
PATH	Operating system pathname
UDID	Universal Device ID
CREATE_DATE	Date and time of adding the disk to the disk group
MOUNT_DATE	Date and time when the disk was mounted by the first instance
REPAIR_TIMER	Seconds remaining until the disk is automatically dropped (0 if not failed)
READS	Total number of I/O read requests to the disk
WRITES	Total number of I/O write requests to the disk
READ_ERRS	Total number of failed I/O read requests to the disk
WRITE_ERRS	Total number of failed I/O write requests to the disk
READ_TIME	Total I/O time for read requests for the disk in hundredths of a second (if TIMED_STATISTICS =TRUE, or 0 if FALSE)
WRITE_TIME	Total I/O time for write requests for the disk in hundredths of a second (if TIMED_STATISTICS =TRUE, or 0 if FALSE)
BYTES_READ	Bytes read from the disk

COLUMN	DESCRIPTION
BYTES_WRITTEN	Bytes written to the disk

v$asm_client - identifies databases using ASM managed disk groups. In a database instance, it has one row for the ASM instance with database has any open ASM files.

COLUMN	DESCRIPTION
GROUP_NUMBER	Disk group number used by the client database instance (foreign key to v$asm_diskgroup)
INSTANCE_NAME	Database client instance identifier
DB_NAME	Unique database instance name
STATUS	Status of the client connection - CONNECTED, DISCONNECTED, BROKEN

v$asm_file - has information on every ADM file in every disk group mounted by the ASM instance. In a database instance, it has no information.

COLUMN	DESCRIPTION
GROUP_NUMBER	Number of the disk group containing the file
FILE_NUMBER	Number of the file within the disk group
COMPOUND_INDEX	32-bit number consisting of disk group number and file number
INCARNATION	Incarnation number for the file
BLOCK_SIZE	File block size in bytes
BLOCKS	Number of blocks in the file
BYTES	Number of bytes in the file

COLUMN	DESCRIPTION
SPACE	Space in bytes allocated to the file
TYPE	File type
REDUNDANCY	Redundancy of the file - MIRROR, PARITY, UNPROT
STRIPED	Type of file striping - FINE, COARSE
CREATION_DATE	File creation date
MODIFICATION_DATE	Last open/close date for writing

v$asm_template - has information on every template present in every disk group mounted by the ASM instance. In a database instance, it has no information.

COLUMN	DESCRIPTION
GROUP_NUMBER	Disk group number (foreign key to v$asm_diskgroup)
ENTRY_NUMBER	Template entry number (Primary key)
REDUNDANCY	Redundancy of the template - MIRROR, PARITY, UNPROT
STRIPE	Striping type for template - FINE, COARSE
SYSTEM	System template or not (Y/N)
NAME	Template name

v$asm_alias - has information on every alias present in every disk group mounted by the ASM instance. In a database instance, it has no information. The structure of *v$asm_alias* has been described earlier under alias names.

v$asm_operation - has information on every active long running ASM operation in the ASM instance. In a database instance, it has no information.

COLUMN	DESCRIPTION
GROUP_NUMBER	Disk group number - Primary key
OPERATION	Operation type - REBAL
STATE	State of the operation - RUNNING, QUEUED
POWER	Power requested for the operation
ACTUAL	Power allocated to the operation
SOFAR	Number of allocation units moved so far by the operation
EST_WORK	Estimated number of allocation units to be moved by the operation
EST_RATE	Estimated number of allocation units being moved per minute by the operation
EST_MINUTES	Estimated amount of time expected for the remainder of the operation to complete in minutes

How Do We Use ASM Files in the Database?

ASM files are Oracle managed files. Unless the ASM files are created using an alias name as studied in previous sections, ASM files are treated as Oracle managed files and deleted when no longer in use.

We can create default disk groups for creation of data files, control files, temp files, redo log files etc. The name of the default disk group will be stored in an initialization parameter file and is not specified during file creation using ASM files.

The following initialization parameters take the ASM filenames or ASM directory names as destination: - *log_archive_dest, log_archive_dest_n,* and *standby_archive_dest.*

These initialization parameters take the ASM filenames as destination: - *control_files, db_create_file_dest, db_create_online_log_dest_n,* and *db_recovery_file_dest.*

The following is an example of how to create a datafile using a default disk group specified by initialization parameter setting. We reset the initialization parameter as follows and create a tablespace.

```
ALTER SYSTEM SET DB_CREATE_FILE_DEST = '+dskgrp01';

CREATE TABLESPACE SALESDATA;
```

The above command will create the SALESDATA tablespace and all data files underneath it on 'dskgrp01'.

You can also use a template to specify the redundancy and striping of datafiles in a disk group. In the above example, use the following commands to use our earlier template of DBAHELPER1.

```
ALTER SYSTEM SET DB_CREATE_FILE_DEST = '+dskgrp01 (DBAHELPER1)';

CREATE TABLESPACE SALESDATA;
```

When ASM creates a datafile the default size is 100MB with auto-extensible feature turned on to unlimited size. However, you can use the SIZE clause to override the default size.

To create the index tablespace for the SALESDATA with just one datafile of 800 MB, use the following command:

```
CREATE TABLESPACE SALESIDX DATAFILE '+dskgrp02' SIZE 800 MB
AUTOEXTEND ON;
```

To create redo log files using ASM files by the same method given above, specify them in initialization parameter file and use the ADD LOGFILE command. The following example creates a log file with a member in each of the 2 disk groups – dskgrp03 and dskgrp04.

```
ALTER SYSTEM SET DB_CREATE_ONLINE_LOG_DEST_1 = '+dskgrp03';
ALTER SYSTEM SET DB_CREATE_ONLINE_LOG_DEST_2 = '+dskgrp04';
ALTER DATABASE ADD LOGFILE;
```

Using ASM to Create a Database

Oracle recommends the use of Database Configuration Assistant (DBCA) to create a new database. However, we can create one manually and using ASM files as follows, with minimum user intervention.

Use the following initialization parameter settings in the database *init.ora* file:

```
DB_CREATE_FILE_DEST = '+dskgrp01'
DB_RECOVERY_FILE_DEST = '+dskgrp02'
CONTROL_FILES = '+dskgrp03'
DB_CREATE_ONLINE_LOG_DEST_1 = '+dskgrp04'
DB_CREATE_ONLINE_LOG_DEST_2 = '+dskgrp05'
LOG_ARCHIVE_DEST = '+dskgrp02'
```

Then, issue the following commands at the SQL prompt connected as a sysdba user to create a new database:

```
STARTUP NOMOUNT;
CREATE DATABASE QASALES ;
```

These commands will create a database with SYSTEM and SYSAUX tablespaces in disk group dskgrp01. It will create a multiplexed online redo with 2 log groups, with one member of each group in dskgrp04 and dskgrp05. The control files will be created in dskgrp03 and dskgrp01. Undo tablespace will be created in dskgrp01, if automatic undo is enabled. Since *log_archive_format* is set to a disk group, *log_archive_format* is ignored and unique filenames for archive logs in *dskgrp02* are generated by the Oracle database.

Conclusion

In this chapter, we have examined the new Oracle Database 10g feature known as ASM. ASM provides the DBA with the capability to manage disks as a high level disk group instead of at the device level. ASM also automatically stripes and balances disks to achieve the maximum in reliability and performance.

Index

About Mike Ault

 *Mike Ault* is one of the leading names in Oracle technology. The author of more than 20 Oracle books and hundreds of articles in national publications, Mike Ault has five Oracle Masters Certificates and was the first popular Oracle author with his landmark book "Oracle7 Administration and Management". Mike also wrote several of the "Exam Cram" books, and enjoys a reputation as a leading author and Oracle consultant.

Mike started working with computers in 1979 right out of a stint in the Nuclear Navy. He began working with Oracle in 1990 and has since become a World Renowned Oracle expert. Mike is currently a Senior Technical Management Consultant and has two wonderful daughters. Mike is kept out of trouble by his wife of 29 years, Susan.

About Mike Reed

When he first started drawing, Mike Reed drew just to amuse himself. It wasn't long, though, before he knew he wanted to be an artist.

Today he does illustrations for children's books, magazines, catalogs, and ads.

He also teaches illustration at the College of Visual Art in St. Paul, Minnesota. Mike Reed says, "Making pictures is like acting — you can paint yourself into the action." He often paints on the computer, but he also draws in pen and ink and paints in acrylics. He feels that learning to draw well is the key to being a successful artist.

Mike is regarded as one of the nation's premier illustrators and is the creator of the popular "Flame Warriors" illustrations at **www.flamewarriors.com**. A renowned children's artist, Mike has also provided the illustrations for dozens of children's books.

Mike Reed has always enjoyed reading. As a young child, he liked the Dr. Seuss books. Later, he started reading biographies and war stories. One reason why he feels lucky to be an illustrator is because he can listen to books on tape while he works. Mike is available to provide custom illustrations for all manner of publications at reasonable prices. Mike can be reached at **www.mikereedillustration.com**.

The Oracle In-Focus Series

The Oracle In-Focus series is a unique publishing paradigm, targeted at Oracle professionals who need fast and accurate working examples of complex issues. Oracle In-Focus books are unique because they have a super-tight focus and quickly provide Oracle professionals with what they need to solve their problems.

Oracle In-Focus books are designed for the practicing Oracle professional. Oracle In-Focus books are an affordable way for all Oracle professionals to get the information they need, and get it fast.

Expert Authors – All Oracle In-Focus authors are content experts and are carefully screened for technical ability and communications skills.

Online Code Depot – All code scripts from Oracle In-Focus are available on the web for instant download. Those who purchase a book will get the URL and password to download their scripts.

Lots of working examples – Oracle In-Focus is packed with working examples and pragmatic tips.

No theory – Practicing Oracle professionals know the concepts, they need working code to get started fast.

Concise – All Oracle In-Focus books are less than 200 pages and get right to-the-point of the tough technical issues.

Tight focus - The Oracle In-Focus series addresses tight topics and targets specific technical areas of Oracle technology.

Affordable – Reasonably priced, Oracle In-Focus books are the perfect solution to challenging technical issues.

http://www.Rampant-Books.com

Conducting the Oracle Job Interview

IT Manager's Guide for Oracle Job Interviews with Oracle Interview Questions

Mike Ault & Don Burleson

ISBN 0-9727513-1-9

Retail Price $16.95 / £10.95

As professional consultants, Don Burleson and Mike Ault have interviewed hundreds of Oracle job candidates. With over four decades of interviewing experience, Ault and Burleson tell you how to quickly identify acceptable Oracle job candidates by asking the right Oracle job interview questions.

Mike Ault and Don Burleson are recognized as the two best-selling Oracle Authors in the world. With combined authorship of over 25 books, Ault & Burleson are the two most respected Oracle authorities on the planet. For the first time ever, Ault & Burleson combine their talents in this exceptional handbook.

Using Oracle job interview questions that are not available to the general public, the IT manager will be able to quickly access the technical ability of any Oracle job candidate. In today's market, there are thousands of under-trained Oracle professionals, and the IT manager must be able to quickly access the true ability of the Oracle job candidate.

www.Rampant-Books.com

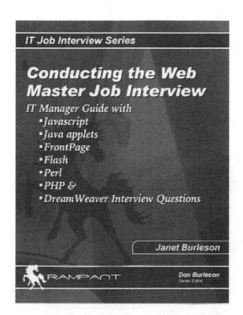

Conducting the Web Master Job Interview

IT Manager Guide with Interview Questions

Janet Burleson

ISBN 0-9745993-1-X

Retail Price $16.95 / £10.95

As a professional web master, Janet Burleson has extensive experience interviewing web master job candidates. With over a decade of interviewing experience, Burleson tell you how to quickly identify acceptable web master job candidates by asking the right web master job interview questions.

This book is the accumulated observations of the author's interviews with hundreds of job candidates. The author provides useful insights into what characteristics make a good web master programmer and offers her accumulated techniques as an aid to interviewing a web master job candidate.

This handy guide has a complete set of web master job interview questions and provides a complete method for accurately assessing the technical abilities of web master job candidates. By using web master job interview questions that only an experienced person knows, your supervisor can ask the right interview questions and fill your web master job with the best qualified web master developer.

www.Rampant-Books.com

Free!
Oracle 10g Senior DBA Reference Poster

This 24 x 36 inch quick reference includes the important data columns and relationships between the DBA views, allowing you to quickly write complex data dictionary queries.

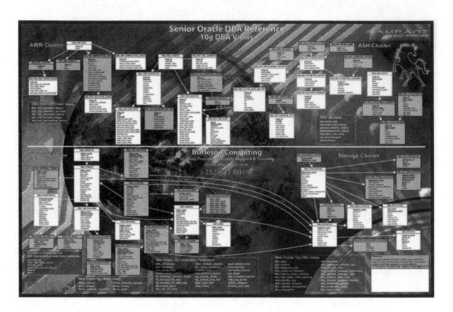

This comprehensive data dictionary reference contains the most important columns from the most important Oracle10g DBA views. Especially useful are the Automated Workload Repository (AWR) and Active Session History (ASH) DBA views.

WARNING - This poster is not suitable for beginners. It is designed for senior Oracle DBAs and requires knowledge of Oracle data dictionary internal structures. You can get your poster at this URL:

www.rampant.cc/poster.htm